The Proposed Constitution of Iran's Elective Monarchy (Elective Shahanshahi)

Reza Hazeli

First Edition 2015
Second Edition 2019
Third Edition 2023
English Version 2024

Mehriran Academy Publications

WWW.MEHRIRAN.ACADEMY

MEHRIRAN.ACADEMY
PUBLICATIONS
MELBOURNE_HOUSTON

Melbourne-Victoria-Australia
Houston-Texas-United States of America

The first and second editions were titled "The Manifesto of the Iranian School of Thought" as political, legal, and managerial principles.

ISBN 978-0-6457178-7-7

ID: Hazeli, Reza, 1979-

Title: The Proposed Constitution of Iran's Elective Monarchy (Elective Shahanshahi)

Publisher Description: Mehriran Academy Publications, Melbourne-Victoria-Australia, Houston-Texas-USA, 2023
WWW.MEHRIRAN.ACADEMY

Format: eBook

ISBN (Print Per.): 978-0-6457178-4-6, 66.6 AUD

ISBN (eBook Per.): 978-0-6457178-5-3, 6.66 AUD

ISBN (eBook Eng.): 978-0-6457178-0-8, 6.66 AUD

ISBN(eBook Eng2): **978-0-6457178-7-7**, 6.66 AUD

ISBN (Print Eng.): 978-0-6457178-2-2, 66.6 AUD

ISBN (Print Eng2): 978-0-6457178-9-1, 66.6 AUD

Status of the listing: CIP

Subtitle: A Parliamentary Republic with Preservation of the Ancient Iranian Political Tradition

Subject: Rights

Subject: Law

Subject: Constitution

DDC: 342

LCC: KMH02050.H39 2023

LCC: KMH02050.A75 2024

Book Design by: Ariana Mehraein (A.H.)

Book Cover by: Oleksander Bilovus

Print: 3rd, 1st, and 2nd versions of the Constitution were published in 2015 and 2019 by the same author in the book "Manifesto of the Iranian School of Thought" as political, legal, and managerial principles.

Edition Number: 2nd

Registration number in Australia: **NLApp108789 (Eng2)** at the National Library of Australia
NLApp104824 (Per) at the National Library of Australia
NLApp108790 (Eng) at the National Library of Australia

Registration number in USA: LCCN: **2024900671 (Eng2)** 2024900677 (Eng) & 2023906120 (Per) & at the Library of Congress of the United States

Editor: Laurie Pitman

Notes: The Original language of this book is Persian (Dari-Parsi (Persian), but it has been written in two alphabets. It is written from right to left in the Dari-Parsi (Persian) alphabet and from left to right in the Iranik alphabet. This is the English translation version of the book done by the author.

NATIONAL LIBRARY OF AUSTRALIA

A catalogue record for this book is available from the National Library of Australia

LIBRARY LIBRARY OF CONGRESS

Library of Congress Control Number:
2024900671

Catalogue-in-Publication

CIP: National Library of Australia

NLA Reference Number: **NLApp108789 (Eng 2),** NLApp108790 (Eng)

CIP: NLApp104824 (Per)

LCCN: Library of Congress **2024900671 (Eng2),** 2024900677 (Eng), 2023906120 (Per)

Format: eBook

Author: Hazeli, Reza, 1979-

Title: The Proposed Constitution of Iran's Elective Monarchy (Elective Shahanshahi)

Subtitle: A Parliamentary republic with preservation of ancient Iranian political tradition

Subject: Law, Constitutional law

Language: English

Alphabet: English

Publisher: Mehriran Academy Publications, Melbourne, Victoria, Australia, 2023. Houston, Texas, USA, 2023.
WWW.MEHRIRAN.ACADEMY

ISBN (Print Per.): 978-0-6457178-4-6

ISBN (eBook Per.): 978-0-6457178-5-3

ISBN (eBook Eng.): 978-0-6457178-0-8

ISBN(eBook Eng2): **978-0-6457178-7-7**

ISBN (Print Eng.): 978-0-6457178-2-2

ISBN (Print Eng2): 978-0-6457178-9-1

DDC: 342

LCC: KMH02050.H39 2023

LCC: KMH02050.A75 2024

Edition Number: 2nd

Print: 3rd

Book Cover by: Oleksander Bilovus

Illustrations by: Ariana Mehraein (A. H.)

Book Design by: Ariana Mehraein (A. H.)

Price: 66.6 AUD (Print), 6.66 AUD (eBook)

NATIONAL LIBRARY OF AUSTRALIA

A catalogue record for this book is available from the National Library of Australia

LIBRARY LIBRARY OF CONGRESS

Library of Congress Control Number: 2024900671

An Offering Dedicated to the Everlasting Essences of the Ancient Iranians and the Iranian Peoples, Tribes, and Nations,
Spanning the Entire Territory of Iran and the Vast Expanse of the Iranian World,
Encompassing (Afghan, Tajik, Khorasani, Persian, Kurdish, Azari, Gilaki, Mazandarani, Baluch, Lor, Bakhtiari, Taleshi, Tat, Alani, Armenian, Sistani, Pashtun, Kumzari, Yaghnabi, Noorestani, Khuzestani, etc.)

An offering dedicated to the eternal spirit of my revered master Zabih Behrooz, who was a genuine expert on Iranian culture and the super-civilization of Indo-Iranian and Europeans.

The following application can be downloaded for typing in Iranik script:

About the Author:

Reza Hazeli is an Iranian origin intellectual, scientist, sociologist, philosopher, and researcher of history, archaeology, and linguistics, as well as a philosophical and political theorist. He studied sociology at Moscow's Lomonosov University, where he earned a master's degree and a Ph.D. He won the gold medal for the best sociologist of the Russian Federation and the Commonwealth of Nations (former Soviet republics) in his undergraduate and graduate programs at Lomonosov University in Moscow. He was also involved in the archaeological excavations of the Russian Academy of Sciences in the field of archaeology at ĒRĀN-WĒZ (BMAC) in Great Khorasan. At the Neishabur Foundation in Tehran, Reza Hazeli studied Shahnameh, Pahlavi, and Avesta languages as a teenager. In addition to his fluency in Dari (Parsi, Tajik), English, and Russian, he is well acquainted with nine languages, which include Kurdish, Spanish, Ukrainian, Bulgarian, Arabic, Sanskrit, Latin, Pahlavi, and Avesta. Additionally, he has completed artificial intelligence research courses at Oxford University in the United Kingdom. As part of his large cultural project, he plans to produce 120 documentary films about the eternal heritage of ancient Iran, including cultural, artistic, musical, literary, scientific, historical, technological, architectural, philosophical, and ritual traditions of ancient Iran. So far, he has produced 21 documentaries. There are dozens of articles that he has authored in Russian, English, and Dari-Parsi (Persian). He has also authored the following books:

1) Iranian Vesta - The Manifesto of the Iranian School of Thought, the Philosophical Manifesto of the School of Thought of Iranism and Iranocracy from a Civilizational Perspective

2) The Secret of Writing - The History and Real Logic of the Creation of the Alphabet

3) The Shahnameh Naderi, the Story of Nader Shah Afshar, the Dynasty of Afshar, and Associated Dynasties

4) The Proposed Constitution of Iran's Elective Monarchy (Elective Shahanshahi) - Parliamentary Republic with Preservation of the Ancient Iranian Political Tradition

5) The Elective Monarchy

Table of Contents

Preface

Despite the fact that the proposed Constitution of Iran's Elective Monarchy (Elective Shahanshahi) is a section of the Iranian Vesta Book and the Manifesto of the Iranian School of Thought to shift the trend of civilization from the Abrahamic civilization to the Indo-Iranian and European super-civilization with the Iranian Revolution, but due to the political distress in Iran and the bewilderment of the political forces and their lack of intellectual order, it is necessary to immediately publish a proposed Constitution for the future of Iran. It was decided to publish this part of this great encyclopedia as soon as possible. Even though many parts of Iran's Elective Monarchy (Elective Shahanshahi) Constitution were released as political and managerial principles and legal principles of the Iranian School of Thought Manifesto in 2015 and 2019, all these laws were scheduled to be published in the third edition of the Iranian School of Thought Manifesto under the name of "Iranian Vesta." But since the third edition of the Manifesto became very bulky and time-consuming, I made up my mind to present this part earlier to fellow countrymen and Iranians and Iranian descendants all over the world so that it would be accepted and be noticed.

Elective Monarchy (Elective Shahanshahi) is a long-lasting political tradition in Iranian and European Indo-Iranian civilizations. Examples in Iran include the election of the first Median king "Deioces," numerous Parthian kings, and also a few Sasanian kings prior to the savage invasion of the Muslim Arabs, as well as the selection of Nader Shah Afshar by the direct vote of more than 20,000 Iranian notables in the Moghan Plain.

The Elective Monarchy (Elective Shahanshahi) also has many precedents in the Indo-Iranian and European super-civilizations, including the ancient Greeks, ancient Romans, ancient Germans and Anglo-Saxons, and ancient Slavs. In this proposed Constitution, this modern political tradition is modernized and mixed with republican patterns.

It is noteworthy that what is intended by the Elective Monarchy (Elective Shahanshahi) in this proposed Constitution is the parliamentary republic in the terminology of political science while preserving some symbolic features of the political and historical tradition of several thousand years of monarchy in Iran, which originated from Iranian national identity and was the key to the survival of Iranian civilization in our eventful history. Obviously, so as to preserve the territorial integrity and national sovereignty of the country and the Iranian identity, some competencies of the President (elected Shah) in the presidential republic were also transferred to the Elected Emperor (elected Shahanshah) to be used in emergency conditions and for a temporary period.

In a nutshell, the Chosen Emperor (elected Shahanshah) in this system is elected by the Mahestan Assembly (Senate) for a limited period of seven years, not more than three times and does not have the right to transfer this title to his/her own personal heirs and children.

In this regime, the Elected Emperor (elected Shahanshah) is a symbol of national unity and the preservation of Iran's existence and Iranian identity, and he/she should be scrupulous in preserving the country's territorial integrity and national sovereignty. This is while the country will be governed by the parliamentary system and its two houses, i.e., the Senate, the House of Representatives, and the Prime Minister himself/herself.

Among the other significant aspects of this Constitution, it should be pointed out that it demonstrates, as well as the rigorous nature of Iranian Laicity, which is stated in the Manifesto of the Iranian School of Thought . This implies that every religion and faith will be isolated from both government and politics, and religious populist parties will not be permitted to function and misuse people's superstitions to achieve power. In this Constitution, religion will be excluded from the three powers of executive, legislative, and judiciary, and education and public forum and the country's civil and criminal laws must be revised based on the doctrine of natural law.

Another characteristic of this Constitution is that it is democratic, based on the theory of Iranian democracy as stated in the Manifesto of the Iranian School of Thought. This implies the Iranian patriarchy of parties that are loyal to Iran and its historical and substantive authenticity are not cosmopolitan and do not desire the destruction and fragmentation of Iran. Moreover, in this Constitution, consideration has been given to the matter of de-centralization in the administration of the country, and it has been proposed to form local governments that lack national sovereignty and territorial integrity for the self-government of the Iranian people and ethnic groups. It is worth mentioning that the local government is not the regional government referred to in Federalism and Confederalism; these governments have national sovereignty and territorial integrity and virtually split the United Country into several nation-states from a legal point of view. Despite the fact that the framework of this Constitution highlights the unified and unitary country of Iran, at the same time, the lack of managerial and executive concentration is obvious in it. Lastly, it is noteworthy that in spite of the fact that the author of this Constitution is not an official jurist, he/she is a philosopher, and he/she is well-informed about the philosophy of law, which is the cornerstone of the science of law. He/she is an expert in Iranian culture and civilization and world politics, and he/she has attempted to prepare a legal masterpiece for the Iranian nation and Iranian civilization and save them from intellectual, identity, and political disorder. This Constitution consists of a text based on the general policy of the Manifesto of the Iranian School of Thought for the transformation of the flow of civilization, together with the common Dari-Parsi (Persian) script, in addition to the natural and scientific Iranik scripts at the same time, which are the outcome of my Professor Zabih Behrouz's ideas and my additional research. It is possible to find a comparative table of the Iranik and Dari (Persian) alphabets in this book's appendixes section for those who are unfamiliar with the Iranik alphabet. Moreover, included in the appendixes are important diagrams that illustrate the political and legal structure of the country, the three branches of government and how they coordinate, and their roles and responsibilities.

Reza Hazeli
Dey 1st, 7761 Mithraic
21 December 2023

The Proposed Constitution of the Iranian School of Thought for the Elective Monarchy (Elective Shahanshahi) Country of Iran

(Parliamentary Republic with Preservation of the Ancient Iranian Political Tradition)

Chapter 1- The Principles of the Legal System

Article 1:

The country of Elective Monarchy (Elective Shahanshahi) of Iran is a laïque and indivisible democratic parliamentary republic under the rule of law, which preserves the political tradition of the Iranian monarchy, in which this ancient tradition has been modernized in such a manner that the king is elected by the representatives of the people for a specified duration. The terms "Elective Monarchy (Elective Shahanshahi) of Iran" and "Iran" have the same legal value in this text.

Article 2:

Human beings and their rights and liberties are the greatest human values. It is the obligation of the government to recognize, respect, and protect the human rights and liberties of humankind and citizens.

Article 3:

1) The united nation of Iran is comprised of various Iranian ethnic groups who have constructed this country over the process of thousands of years of history and have been sacrificed for it, who have constructed Iranian identity and Iranian languages, who have Iranian festivals, traditions, and cultures, and who are the exclusive source of power in Iran's Elective Monarchy (Elective Shahanshahi).

2) The people exert their power directly and through governmental institutions in the electoral process.

3) The most direct manifestation of the people's power is through referendums and free elections.

4) In the monarchy country of Iran, no one can exclusively take power and usurpation of governmental power is forbidden by law.

Article 4:

1) The national sovereignty of the monarchy country of Iran encompasses the entire territory of this country and is superior to global sovereignty.

2) The Constitution of Iran and its other laws prevail all over the country.

3) The Elective Monarchy (Elective Shahanshahi) of Iran guarantees the unity, inviolability, and territorial integrity of its territory.

Article 5:

1) The Elective Monarchy (Elective Shahanshahi) of Iran consists of the Iranian provincial kingdoms and their local governments, which are equal members of the Senate.

2) The Elective Monarchy (Elective Shahanshahi) of Iran has a Constitution and other laws, and the laws of the provincial kingdoms and their governments and local assemblies must be in accordance with the Constitution of the whole country and in the same direction.

3) The structure of Iran's Elective Monarchy (Elective Shahanshahi) is based on the integrity of the state, the authority of the state, the distribution of authority and power among state organizations and institutions of state power and local governments, and the equality and human and Iranian rights of the Iranian people.

4) All provincial local governments are equal in relation to the national institutions of governmental power.

Article 6:

1) Citizenship of the Elective Monarchy (Elective Shahanshahi) of Iran is suspended or obtained throughout the country, but the rights of citizenship are the same and equal independent of the reasons for obtaining it.

2) Every citizen of the Iranian monarchy has all the rights and liberties throughout its territory and has the same responsibilities as others for the duties listed in the country's Constitution.

3) None of the citizens of the Iranian monarchy can be deprived of their citizenship or coerced into changing their citizenship, although citizenship itself can be abolished.

Article 7:

1) The Iranian Elective Monarchy (Elective Shahanshahi) is a social state whose aim is to create dignified living conditions and free human development. The provision of the moral and physical needs of man is followed by the provision of his/her and society's welfare.

2) In Iran's Elective Monarchy (Elective Shahanshahi), people's work and health are protected. The guarantee of the minimum wage and the government's support for families and parents of children, the aged, and the handicapped are provided. The social service system is developed, and pensions and other social security guarantees are made.

Article 8:

1) The Elective Monarchy (Elective Shahanshahi) of Iran ensures the integrity of the economic environment; the free flow of goods, services, and capital; the promotion of competitive activities; and the freedom of economic activity.

2) Private, public, social (cooperative), and other forms of ownership are recognized.

Article 9:

Land and other natural resources in Iran's Elective Monarchy (Elective Shahanshahi) are used and promoted as the foundation of life and activity of the people living in its territories.

Article 10:

The power of government in the Iranian Elective Monarchy (Elective Shahanshahi) shall be executed based on the separation of legislative, executive, and judicial powers. The legislative, executive, and judiciary powers are independent.

Article 11:

1) Sovereignty in the Iranian Elective Monarchy (Elective Shahanshahi) is carried out by the Elected Emperor (elected Shahanshah), the Prime Minister, the Iran Zamin Association or Parliament (Senate and House of Representatives), the Iranian Elective Monarchy (Elective Shahanshahi) Government, and the Iranian Elective Monarchy Courts.

2) The governmental power of the Iranian Elective Monarchy (Elective Shahanshahi) is carried out by the governmental organizations and their members under the framework of the law.

3) The separation of powers and authority among the governmental institutions of the Iranian Elective Monarchy (Elective Shahanshahi) Government is based on the law and the treaties of the Parliament (House of Representatives and Senate) and other governmental treaties dealing with the separation of powers.

Article 12:

Local governments with Iranian identity are recognized and guaranteed in the Elective Monarchy (Elective Shahanshahi) of Iran.

Article 13:

1) Ideological variety is affirmed in Iran's Elective Monarchy (Elective Shahanshahi).

2) No cosmopolitan and non-national ideology (including Islamic, communist, extreme globalist, mondialist, and Abrahamic) can exist as a state ideology.

3) Political diversity and a multi-party system are allowed in Iran's Elective Monarchy (Elective Shahanshahi).

4) Public and popular associations are equal before the law.

5) It is forbidden to establish and operate social organizations that aim to change by force the foundations of the legal system and the principle of laicity, to breach the integrity and territorial integrity of the Iranian Elective Monarchy (Elective Shahanshahi), to endanger its security, to create military units, and to instigate social, racial, and religious enmity.

6) In Iran's Elective Monarchy (Elective Shahanshahi), political parties, military, and law enforcement forces are national, not provincial, regional, or local.

7) Ethnic factions are forbidden in the Iran Zamin Association (the two houses of the Iranian Parliament).

Article 14:

1) Iran's Elective Monarchy (Elective Shahanshahi) is a non-religious and laïque state; thus, no religion can be a state or mandatory religion. In Iran's Elective Monarchy (Elective Shahanshahi), religion must be separated from the institution of government, politics, legislation, judiciary, public culture, education, and higher education. The formation of religious parties or parties of a religious nature is forbidden, and the activity of religious institutions is only permitted in the private sphere or in religious venues such as mosques and Hussainiyas.

2) Governmental assemblies are separate from the government and are equal in front of the law.

3) The activities of parties that endanger the national sovereignty and territorial integrity of the Iranian Elective Monarchy (Elective

Shahanshahi), including communist cosmopolitan and extreme globalist parties or secessionist parties, are not permitted.

Article 15:

1) The Constitution of the Elective Monarchy (Elective Shahanshahi) of Iran has great legal capacity and is enforced by direct measures throughout the territory of the Elective Monarchy (Elective Shahanshahi) of Iran. Laws and legal documents in Iran must not contradict the Constitution of the entire country.

2) State and government organizations, local governments, officials, citizens, and their assemblies are obliged to abide by the Constitution of the Elective Monarchy (Elective Shahanshahi) of Iran and its other regulations.

3) Regulations must be officially announced. Non-published regulations are not in effect. Legal documents related to human rights and liberties and the obligations of individuals and citizens are not executable unless they are officially published for public knowledge.

4) Internationally recognized norms of international law and international treaties of the Elective Monarchy (Elective Shahanshahi) of Iran are part of its legal system. If an international treaty specifies Iran's Elective Monarchy (Elective Shahanshahi)

other than the standards approved in the Constitution, the international treaty will not be valid and should not be approved by the country's Parliament (House of Representatives and Senate).

Article 16:

1) The provisions of this chapter constitute the foundations of the legal system of Iran's Elective Monarchy (Elective Shahanshahi) and shall not be amended except in the order specified in the Constitution.

2) The future provisions of this Constitution shall not be in contradiction with the principles of Iran's Elective Monarchy (Elective Shahanshahi) legal system as stated in this chapter.

Chapter 2- Human and Citizen Rights and Liberties

Article 17:

1) Human and citizen rights and liberties are affirmed and guaranteed in the Elective Monarchy (Elcctive Shahanshahi) of Iran.

2) Human rights and liberties are inseparable and are realized from the day of birth of every human being.

3) The exercise of human and citizen rights and liberties should not interfere with the rights and liberties of others.

Article 18:

Human and citizen rights and liberties are directly applicable. They determine the nature, meaning, and method of executing laws and the activities of the legislative, executive, and local authorities, and the judicial system guarantees their realization.

Article 19:

1) Everyone is equal before the law and the court.

2) The government guarantees equality of rights and liberties regardless of gender, race, nationality, language, religion,

property and official position, place of residence, religion, beliefs, and membership in social organizations and other conditions.

3) Men and women have equal rights and liberties and equal opportunities to implement them.

Article 20:

1) Everyone has the right to live.

2) Capital punishment has no place in Iran's Elective Monarchy (Elective Shahanshahi). Identification and physical elimination of the enemies of the country and the Iranian identity, values, and civilization, whose betrayal of the Iranian civilization has been proven, can be done in necessary cases with the discretion of the secret courts of the Elective Monarchy Secret Service of Iran or the Elective Monarchy Guard Secret Service of Iran.

Article 21:

1) Human dignity shall be protected. Nothing may be the cause of human degradation.

2) No one shall be subjected to torture, cruelty, or any other form of humiliation or punishment. No one shall be subjected to medical and scientific experiments without his/her voluntary consent or forced to undergo injections under any excuse.

Article 22:

1) Everyone has the right to liberty and private immunity.

2) Imprisonment and attachment of persons shall be permitted only on the basis of a court decision. No one may be imprisoned for more than 48 hours in the absence of a court verdict.

Article 23:

1) Everyone has the right to privacy, personal and family secrecy, and protection of his/her good name and reputation.

2) Privacy of correspondence, telephone conversations, postal, and other communications is the right of everyone. These rights may be restricted only on the basis of a court decision.

Article 24:

1) It is prohibited to collect, store, use, and publish information on people's private lives without their permission.

2) The central and local governments and their officials shall not allow anyone access to documents and papers relating to individual rights and freedoms unless otherwise provided by law.

Article 25:

A person's home is immune. No one shall have the right to enter a person's home against the will of its occupants, except in cases prescribed by law or by court decree.

Article 26:

1) Everyone has the right to determine and express his/her Iranian ethnic identity. No one may be compelled to determine and express his/her ethnic identity.

2) All people have the right to use their native Iranian languages with free decisions for conversation, education, private training, and creativity.

Article 27:

1) All persons legally residing in the Elective Monarchy (Elective Shahanshahi) of Iran have the right to move freely and select their place of residence.

2) Everyone is free to exit their country. Citizens of the Iranian Elective Monarchy (Elective Shahanshahi) have the right to return to the country freely.

Article 28:

Freedom of belief and freedom of religion, including the right to pursue a religion individually or collectively or to disbelieve in religion, is guaranteed by free choice for everybody; however, because of the crimes of Abrahamic religions, especially Islam, against Iranian culture and civilization throughout history, these religions do not have the right to propagate in Iran's Elective Monarchy (Elective Shahanshahi), although they have the right to exist.

Article 29:

1) The right to freedom of conscience and speech is guaranteed to all individuals.

2) Advertising and incitement to create social, racial, and ethnic hatred and enmity are forbidden.

3) No one shall be compelled to express or deny his/her opinions and beliefs.

4) Everyone shall have the right and liberty to receive, impart, produce, and publish information by any lawful means unless such information is part of state secrets. The comprehensive list of information that constitutes state secrets shall be determined by law.

5) Freedom of the mass media shall be guaranteed, and any censorship shall be forbidden.

Article 30:

1) All persons shall have the right to form associations, including the right to form labor unions for the protection of their interests. Freedom of action of public labor unions shall be secured.

2) No one may be held accountable or condemned for joining or remaining in a labor union.

Article 31:

The citizens of the Elective Monarchy (Elective Shahanshahi) of Iran have the right to peaceful and unarmed assembly and to hold marches, meetings, demonstrations, and strikes.

Article 32:

1) The citizens of the Iranian Elective Monarchy (Elective Shahanshahi) have the right to participate directly or indirectly through their representatives in the management of governmental affairs.

2) The citizens of the Iranian Elective Monarchy (Elective Shahanshahi) have the right to elect and be elected to

governmental organizations and local governments, as well as to engage in referendums.

3) Citizens who have been found incompetent by the court, as well as citizens who are in prison based on a court decision, are deprived of the right to vote and be elected.

4) Citizens of Iran's Elective Monarchy (Elective Shahanshahi) have the right to equal access to governmental services.

5) Citizens of Iran's Elective Monarchy (Elective Shahanshahi) have the right to participate in judicial proceedings.

Article 33:

Citizens of the Iranian Elected Monarchy (Elective Shahanshahi) have the right to approach governmental bodies and local governments and submit their demands collectively or individually.

Article 34:

1) All individuals have the right to use their abilities and property for economic and other activities not forbidden by law.

2) Economic activities to form monopolies and illegal competition are not permitted.

Article 35:

1) The right to private ownership shall be safeguarded by law.

2) All persons have the right to private ownership and may use it individually or collectively.

3) No one may be deprived of his/her property without the decision of a tribunal.

4) The right of inheritance shall be guaranteed.

Article 36:

1) Citizens and their associations have the right to private ownership of land.

2) Ownership, exploitation, and management of land and other natural resources shall be free for their owners, provided that it does not lead to the destruction of the environment and contradict the rights and interests of other persons.

3) The requirements and regulations for the exploitation of land shall be determined by law.

Article 37:

1) Labor is free. Everyone has the right to freely use his/her working capacity and choose the kind of work he/she wants to do.

2) Forced labor is forbidden.

3) Everybody has the right to safety and health at work, to equal and minimum wages determined by law, and to protection against unemployment.

4) The right to settle collective, individual, and labor disputes employing strategies and solutions established by law and the right to strike shall be recognized.

5) Everyone has the right to rest, and for those who work according to the contract, the duration of work, holidays, and vacations will be determined and guaranteed by the law.

Article 38:

1) The family, mother, and children shall be protected by the State.

2) The care and upbringing of children shall be the equal obligation of parents.

3) Children over the age of 18 must take care of their disabled parents.

Article 39:

1) Social security shall be guaranteed to all persons in old age, including sickness and disability, inability to work for raising children, and other cases determined by law.

2) Retirement pensions and social security income supplements shall be determined by law.

3) Voluntary social security insurance shall be developed by providing supplementary forms of social security and charity.

Article 40:

1) Everyone has the right to adequate housing, and no one shall be arbitrarily deprived of his/her housing.

2) State and local authorities shall develop housing and create prerequisites for the realization of the right to adequate housing.

3) Low-income persons and citizens referred to in the law shall receive free housing or reasonable rent from municipalities and other sources of housing supply in accordance with the standards set forth in the law.

Article 41:

1) Everyone has the right to health protection and medical services. Medical services in public and municipal institutions shall be financed through the relevant budgets, insurance payments, and other procedures and shall be provided to citizens free of charge.

2) The government provides health care and empowerment programs for the people of the Elective Monarchy (Elective Shahanshahi) of Iran, and measures are taken to develop and promote public, urban, and private health services. There are programs to develop and promote health and hygiene, to develop physical education and sports, and to enhance general health.

3) If governmental authorities conceal the facts and situations that threaten people's lives and health, they will be prosecuted under the law.

Article 42:

All people have the right to a suitable environment and reliable information about its status, and in case of damage to their health and property due to environmental violations, they have the right to compensation.

Article 43:

1) Everyone has the right to education.

2) Public and free access of people to preschool, primary, and secondary education in public and municipal educational institutions shall be guaranteed.

3) Everyone has the right to free access to higher education in public and municipal educational institutions on the basis of competition.

4) Basic public education shall be free of charge. Parents and guardians shall ensure their children's access to basic public education.

5) The Ministry of Culture of the Elective Monarchy (Elective Shahanshahi) of Iran determines the state's educational standards and supports various forms of education and self-learning.

Article 44:

1) The freedom of literary, artistic, scientific, and technical creation and its various forms is guaranteed.

2) Everyone has the right to participate in cultural life in order to acquire cultural values.

3) All people are committed to preserving cultural and historical heritage and supporting historical and cultural works.

Article 45:

1) The government's support for the rights and liberties of people and citizens is secured in Iran's Elective Monarchy (Elective Shahanshahi).

2) The people may defend their rights and liberties by any means not forbidden by law.

Article 46:

1) Judicial defense of the rights and liberties of individuals is guaranteed.

2) Decisions and measures of state authorities may be appealed in court.

3) Everybody has the right to appeal to international institutions for the defense of human rights and liberties according to the international agreements of the Elective Monarchy (Elective Shahanshahi) of Iran if the governmental means available in the country for their legal protection have not been effective.

Article 47:

1) No one may be deprived of the right to have his/her case heard in court and by a judge, according to his/her discretion.

2) The person accused of committing a crime has the right to demand that his/her case be heard by a jury in the cases provided for by law.

Article 48:

1) The right to specialized legal assistance is guaranteed to all persons in the process of a trial, and this assistance is free in the cases provided by law.

2) Every imprisoned person under arrest, who is accused of committing a crime, has the right to legal assistance and counseling from the moment of his/her arrest, imprisonment, or indictment.

Article 49:

1) Every person accused of committing a crime is innocent until his/her crime is proven in accordance with the law and confirmed by a final court decision.

2) The accused does not have to prove his/her innocence.

3) Irresolvable doubts about the accused's crime shall be interpreted in his/her favor.

Article 50:

1) No one shall be tried twice for the same crime.

2) Evidence obtained through violation of the rules may not be used in the trial.

3) Anyone convicted of a crime shall have the right to appeal the verdict to a higher court or to ask for pardon or reduction of punishment, as provided by law.

Article 51:

1) No one may be compelled to testify against himself/herself, his/her spouse and close relatives, or other persons determined by the law of the state.

2) The law shall determine other cases of suspension of the obligation to testify.

Article 52:

The law shall protect the rights of victims of crime and abuse of power, and the government shall provide them with access to the courts and compensation for their losses.

Article 53:

All persons have the right to receive compensation for damages caused by illegal measures or failure to act in a timely manner by governmental organizations and their officials.

Article 54:

1) A law that is applied in a timely manner or that increases punishment shall not be applied retroactively.

2) A person cannot be punished for an act that was not a crime at the time it was committed, and if the punishment is reduced or canceled after the crime has been committed, the new law shall be applied.

Article 55:

1) Referring to the fundamental rights and liberties of the Iranian Elective Monarchy (Elective Shahanshahi) shall not be interpreted as denying or limiting other universally recognized human rights and liberties.

2) Laws that violate or restrict human rights and liberties shall not be passed in Iran's Elective Monarchy (Elective Shahanshahi).

3) The rights and freedoms of human beings and citizens may not be restricted by laws except to the extent required to protect the foundations of the legal and moral system; the health, legal, and lawful interests of other people; and to guarantee the defense of the country and the security of the government.

Article 56:

1) In a state of emergency, in order to ensure the safety of citizens and to protect the legal system in accordance with the Constitution, special restrictions may be imposed on human rights and liberties by determining the limits and duration of their validity.

2) A state of emergency may be declared in the whole of the Elected Monarchy (Elective Shahanshahi) of Iran or some specific zones under the conditions specified in the Constitution.

3) The rights and liberties mentioned in Part One (Articles 20, 21, and 23), Part Two (Articles 24, 28, 34, and 40), and Articles 46-54 of the Constitution of the Elective Monarchy (Elective Shahanshahi) of Iran cannot be restricted.

Article 57:

All individuals are obligated to pay the taxes and duties established by law. New tax regulations or regulations that are unfavorable to taxpayers shall not be applied retroactively.

Article 58:

Everyone is obliged to preserve nature and the environment and to use natural resources carefully.

Article 59:

1) Defending the Iranian homeland and civilization is the duty of all citizens of the Elective Monarchy (Elective Shahanshahi) of Iran.

2) Every citizen must participate in military service following the regulations of the law.

Article 60:

Every citizen of the Iranian Elective Monarchy (Elective Shahanshahi) can fully perform his/her rights and duties as of the age of 18.

Article 61:

1) The citizens of Iran's Elective Monarchy (Elective Shahanshahi) cannot be expelled from the country or extradited to another country.

2) The Iranian Elective Monarchy (Elective Shahanshahi) ensures the defense and protection of its citizens abroad.

Article 62:

1) Every citizen of Iran may have the nationality of the country or other countries (the plurality of nationality) based on the law or international agreements of the Elective Monarchy (Elective Shahanshahi) of Iran.

2) Holding the nationality of another country does not diminish the rights and liberties of the citizens of the government of the Elective Monarchy (Elective Shahanshahi) of Iran, nor does it exempt them from fulfilling the duties deriving from the nationality of the government of the Elective Monarchy (Elective Shahanshahi) of Iran unless provided for by the law or international treaties of Iran.

3) Foreign citizens and stateless persons in the Elective Monarchy (Elective Shahanshahi) of Iran have the rights and duties of

Iranian citizens, with the exception of the situations specified by the law or international treaties of Iran.

Article 63:

1) The Elective Monarchy (Elective Shahanshahi) of Iran grants political asylum to foreign nationals and stateless individuals based on international standards and norms.

2) The extradition of people based on political crimes is not allowed in the Elected Monarchy (Elective Shahanshahi) of Iran. The extradition of people accused of committing crimes, as well as the extradition of convicts to face their punishment in other countries, is carried out in accordance with the law and international treaties.

Article 64:

The contents of this chapter constitute the basis of the legal status of persons in the Elective Monarchy (Elective Shahanshahi) of Iran and cannot be modified except in accordance with the provisions of this Constitution.

Chapter 3- Iranian Elective Monarchy (Elective Shahanshahi): Trans-Citizens' Trans-Humanist and Trans-Mankind Rights

Article 65:

Any human being regardless of race whose technology temporarily or permanently increases or decreases his/her mental and physical abilities in a manner inseparable from his/her foundation and body shall be considered a trans-human or trans-mankind.

Article 66:

Technologies that temporarily or permanently transform human beings into trans-humans by embedding in the body include but are not limited to the following: information technology, artificial intelligence technology, electronic technology, mechanical technology, chemical technology, genetic technology, biological and molecular technology, and medical and pharmaceutical technology.

Article 67:

A robot is distinguished from a trans-human and is an electromechanical or molecular genetic device that does not have a human origin.

Article 68:

The rights of humans are equal to those of trans-humans if the trans-human is of human origin and not of robotic origin.

Article 69:

The robot, whatever it is, has no real or juristic personality, and its work and abilities belong to the human or trans-human who owns it.

Article 70:

1) Artifacts and technological products, as soon as they are placed permanently or temporarily in the human body, are considered part of its organs and lose the intellectual rights and patents of the real or juristic personality of their maker. These rights will belong to the trans-human, with no right to sell them to anyone.

2) A trans-human of human origin, even if more than 50% of his/her body consists of technologies with registered intellectual rights, has rights that are equal to the rights of a free and natural human being, and no real or juristic person has the right to possess him/her.

Article 71:

1) The robot shall not harm human beings or trans-human beings or cause harm to human beings or trans-human beings by inaction.

2) The robot must obey the commands of humans or trans-humans unless those commands contradict paragraph one of this article.

3) The robot should defend its existence, as long as this existence does not contradict the first and second paragraphs of this article.

Article 72:

Governments and centers of power do not have the right to violate the rights of humans and trans-humans by employing robots, thus Iran's Elective Monarchy (Elective Shahanshahi) is no exception to this rule.

Article 73:

Governments and centers of power, including the Elective Monarchy (Elective Shahanshahi) of Iran, do not have the right to discriminate between humans and trans-humans in any manner and under any excuse.

Article 74:

Governments and centers of power, including the Elective Monarchy (Elective Shahanshahi) of Iran, do not have the right to restrict the right to sovereignty and democracy of humans under the pretext of their inferiority to trans-humans.

Article 75:

The rights of a female trans-human are equal to those of a male trans-human.

Article 76:

The rights of a human child are equal to the rights of a trans-human child.

Article 77:

1) Every trans-human who acquires the citizenship of the Elective Monarchy (Elective Shahanshahi) of Iran is deemed to be a trans-citizen.

2) The rights of a trans-citizen of the Elective Monarchy (Elective Shahanshahi) of Iran are equal to the rights of its citizens.

Article 78:

The Universal Declaration of Human Rights shall apply to trans-human of human origin.

Article 79:

The transition from humanity to trans-humanity must be voluntary with the consent of human beings, and a person cannot be forced to enter trans-humanity with or without his/her knowledge under any excuse or duress, including the excuse of various epidemics and compulsory vaccinations.

Article 80:

The process of transition from humanity to trans-humanism should be transparent, and detailed information regarding the output of substances that cause changes in the human body should be debated and voted on by the public and experts before testing on humans and implementing them; these products should not be monopolized by the centers of power and their affiliated companies for the exploitation of human beings and imposed on the public in a non-transparent, coercive, and uninformed manner.

Article 81:

In the event of economic, social, cultural, and political damage to humans and citizens in competition with trans-humans or robots, governments, including the Elective Monarchy (Elective Shahanshahi) of Iran, are committed to compensating the minimum losses of humans and citizens.

Article 82:

In the event of widespread unemployment and loss of human ability to compete with trans-humans and robots, governments, including the Elective Monarchy (Elective Shahanshahi) of Iran, are obligated to pay minimum monthly unemployment benefits and housing rights and provide free education and health care to humans and citizens who have been disabled from competing with trans-humans and robots during the Fourth Industrial Revolution.

Article 83:

Neither Iran's Elective Monarchy (Elective Shahanshahi), government or power center, nor the natural or juristic person has the right to use "trans-mankind" technologies to diminish the abilities of humans and citizens with the purpose of dominating, exploiting, and restricting them.

Article 84:

The "public good" in trans-mankind and the technologies leading to it will be determined by "collective intelligence" and transparent expert and public debate, not by secret power centers, the Vatican, governments, or multinational and major global corporations.

Article 85:

Any kind of robot, even if it is a biological or molecular robot and has achieved self-awareness, is still a robot and is not considered a trans-mankind or mankind.

Article 86:

Robots, even if they successfully pass the Turing test and humans and trans-humans are unable to recognize their identity, are still considered robots and not humans or trans-humans.

Chapter 4- The Rights of the Founders, Proprietors, and Heirs of Iran and Iranian Civilization

Article 87:

Iran is the mainstay of the Iranian civilized countries and the oldest natural country, which has existed from the very beginning of history, even before the concept of the nation-state, and has no independent history. Political Iran has always resurrected after stages of collapse and continued its existence along with the immortal and unconquerable cultural Iran.

Article 88:

The historical proprietors of Iran are the people with Iranian identity. Iran, as its name indicates, is the land of the Iranian tribes who established it, and throughout the history of Iranian culture, they established Iranian languages and Iranian history, and they were murdered and sacrificed for Iranian identity.

Article 89:

Iran is the foremost country of the Iranian civilization, an integral component of the Indo-Iranian and European civilizations. The Islamic-Abrahamic deviations caused in this country must be eliminated through the Iranian identity revolution, and this country should be restored to its original civilizational route.

Article 90:

Iranian identity is based on four factors: common history from ancient times to the present, Iranian languages are considered a part of Indo-Iranian and European languages, cultural anthropology and biological anthropology, and any tribe possessing at minimum two of the above four factors has an Iranian identity.

Article 91:

Iran, as its name implies, is the historical country of the Iranian nation and Indo-Iranian and European guests and not the land of immigrants and people who do not have Indo-Iranian and European identity.

Article 92:

Immigrants or non-Iranian assailants and their children who were born in Iran over the history do not have the right to the lands of

Iran and do not have political and cultural rights. These individuals only have the right to citizenship and are able to become Iranian by accepting the Iranian identity or go back to their original countries.

Article 93:

The historical and ancient owners of Iran do not accept the logic of violence, and therefore, the culture and religion of the aggressor, Abrahamic Islam, which was imposed on them by killing and massacring Iranians, is not part of Iranian culture and identity, since it has a foreign aggressor father who is a usurper and a felon.

Article 94:

Iran towards other Iranian territories, including Tajikistan and Afghanistan, occupied Kurdistan in Turkey, Iraq, Syria, Ossetia, and Alania; occupied Balochistan in Pakistan; occupied Kumzar south of the Strait of Hormuz, Bahrain, Baku, Armenia, Talesh; and occupied Tatestan outside Iran. has the position of a loving and compassionate mother for her children.

Article 95:

Iran does not accept the forcible entry of non-Iranian nations and countries into Iranian territories or belonging to Iranian civilization and identity; and in case of conflict between some

Iranian tribes and nations, it must maintain its position of neutrality and try to settle the differences of its children in a just way.

Article 96:

Iran is the homeland of the Aryans and the heir of their identity and civilization in Airyanem Vaejah; consequently, the actual and natural intellectual property of the Indo-Iranian Aryan civilization zones abroad belongs to Iran.

Article 97:

All Iranian tribes and nations out of Iran must have supervisors in the House of Representatives and Mahestan of Iran in proportion to their population to the whole population of the Iranian civilized nation.

Article 98:

1) For the revival of the unified soul of the Iranian civilization and identity, it is essential to establish cultural, political, economic,

and military unions among the Iranian peoples, tribes, and nations with Iran as the center.

2) All Iranian territories and countries, tribes, and nations are regarded as elements of Iran and Iranian civilization, and the Elective Monarchy (Elective Shahanshahi) country of Iran is obligated to protect and support them and release the occupied territories.

Chapter 5- Elective Monarchy (Elective Shahanshahi) of Iran (Parliamentary Republic with the Preservation of the Ancient Iranian Political Tradition)

Article 99:

1) The Elective Monarchy (Elective Shahanshahi) country of Iran is a unified and laicist country on the foundation of Iranian laicism as stipulated in the Manifesto of the Iranian School of Thought, having the right to national sovereignty and territorial integrity in consideration of human history; however, it is decentralized and composed of the following provinces, which are ruled by local governments (local kingdoms) with no national sovereignty and territorial integrity:

1- Atropatene (East Azerbaijan)

2- Urmia (West Azerbaijan)

3- Ardabil

4- Sepahan (Isfahan)

5- Alborz

6- Arata (Ilam)

7- Tehran

8- Bakhtiari (Chaharmahal and Bakhtiari)

9- Khorasan (South and Razavi)

10- Khorasan Afshar (Northern)

11- Khuzestan

12- Zanjan

13- Semnan

14- Sistan

15- Balochistan

16- Pars (Fars and Bushehr)

17- Persian Gulf (Abu Musa, Greater Tunb and Lesser Tunb, and occupied Aryan island in UAE)

18- Caspian (Qazvin)

19- Qom

20- Ardalan (Rojhalat Kurdistan)

21- Kerman

22- Kermanshah

23- Kohgiluyeh (Kohgiluyeh and Boyer Ahmad)

24- Gilan

25- Lorestan

26- Mazandaran (Mazandaran and Golestan)

27- Arak (Central)

28- Hormozgan

29- Hamedan

30- Yazd

2) The access of new provinces from other countries and the establishment of new provinces inside the country of the Elective Monarchy (Elective Shahanshahi) of Iran shall be carried out under the provisions of the Constitution.

3) The provinces of the Elective Monarchy (Elective Shahanshahi) of Iran are regarded as part of Iran and are indivisible from the motherland.

4) The provincial kingdom (provincial local government) is the second stage of country division in the unified country of Iran. A *province* means a territory having a specific geographical area, created by combining some neighboring cities following political,

historical, social, cultural, ethnic, economic, and natural circumstances.

Article 100:

The unitary country of Iran will consist of eight economic zones. Each economic zone will include some provinces with common geographical, historical, cultural, transportation, and economic infrastructures. These zones will have common development schedules in the country's Planning and Budget Organization, and the macroeconomic and country plans will be implemented by the ministries of the central government and the country's Planning and Budget Organization in cooperation with the local governments of the provinces of these zones. Each economic zone shall be administered by the representative of the same economic zone in the Planning and Budget Organization and the Ministry of Interior Affairs of the central government. The representatives of the economic zones in the central government must be natives of the same economic zone, and the representative post of the economic zone must be alternated among the representatives of the provinces of the same economic zone in one-year periods. This representative shall be elected by the local assembly of each province of each economic zone from its members for a one-year term. The representative of each economic zone in the central government is called "Kay." These economic zones are 1) Pars Zone, 2) Khorasan Zone, 3) Caspian Zone, 4) Northern Mad Zone, 5) Southern Mad Zone, 6) Western Mad Zone, 7) Sepahan Zone, and 8) Capital Zone.

1) Pars Economic Zone consists of the provinces of Pars, Persian Gulf, Hormozgan, and Kerman.

2) Khorasan Economic Zone consists of the provinces of Khorasan Afshar, Khorasan, Sistan, and Balochistan.

3) Caspian Economic Zone consists of the provinces of Gilan, Mazandaran, Alborz, Semnan, Ardabil, and Caspian.

4) Northern Mad Economic Zone consists of the provinces of Atropatene and Zanjan.

5) Southern Mad Economic Zone consists of the Arak province.

6) Western Mad Economic Zone consists of the provinces of Urmia, Ardalan (Kurdistan Rojhalat), Hamedan, Kermanshah, Lorestan, Arata (Ilam), Khuzestan, Bakhtiari, and Kohgiluyeh.

7) Sepahan Economic Zone consists of the provinces of Sepahan, Yazd, and Qom.

8) Capital Economic Zone consists of the Tehran province.

Article 101:

1) The Elective Monarchy (Elective Shahanshahi) territory of Iran encompasses the territory of all economic zones and provinces or local kingdoms and internal waters and territorial sea and its upper space.

2) The Elective Monarchy (Elective Shahanshahi) of Iran has its own sovereign right and exerts its powers in the Iranian plateau, economic zones, and provincial kingdoms in compliance with the Constitution and the norms of international law.

3) The borders between the provinces of the Elective Monarchy (Elective Shahanshahi) of Iran may be modified on the basis of their mutual agreement.

Article 102:

1) The Dari (Persian) language with a Persian accent shall be the state and official language and the language of state and government education throughout the Elective Monarchy (Elective Shahanshahi) of Iran.

2) The provinces are entitled to determine their state language, which has Iranian or at least Indo-Iranian and European origins

and does not contradict the identity and authenticity of Iran's history and is not the language of invading tribes or non-Iranian immigrants. These languages are utilized in the governmental organizations of the relevant provinces along with the state and official language of Iran's Elective Monarchy (Elective Shahanshahi).

3) Iran's Elective Monarchy (Elective Shahanshahi) ensures the right of all people to maintain their native languages, even if these languages are of assailant and usurping tribes and non-Iranian immigrants to Iran.

Article 103:

The Iranian Elective Monarchy (Elective Shahanshahi) ensures the rights of all native peoples with a small population according to the internationally approved principles and regulations and the norms of international law and international treaties of Iran.

Article 104:

1) The description and arrangements for the official application of the Elective Monarchy (Elective Shahanshahi) of Iran's vexillum, emblem, and national anthem shall be stipulated by the Constitution of Iran.

2) The capital of the Elective Monarchy (Elective Shahanshahi) of Iran is the city of Tehran (ancient Raga), the status of the center will be determined by law.

Article 105:

The authorities of the Elective Monarchy (Elective Shahanshahi) of Iran are:

A) Enacting and revising the Constitution of the Elective Monarchy (Elective Shahanshahi) of Iran and domestic laws, and to supervise their implementation.

B) Determining the structure and territory of the Iranian Elective Monarchy (Elective Shahanshahi).

C) Regulating and protecting the rights and liberties of humans, trans-humans, citizens, trans-citizens, tribes with Iranian identity, the Iranian nation, Iranian civilization, and Iranian identity and citizenship in the Elective Monarchy (Elective Shahanshahi) of Iran.

D) Establishing the system of legislative, executive, and judicial bodies, their organizational structure and their functions, and the foundation of the governmental entities of the Elective Monarchy (Elective Shahanshahi) of Iran.

E) Providing ownership of the state properties of the Iranian Elective Monarchy (Elective Shahanshahi) and their administration.

F) Determining the basis of national policies and plans in the areas of governmental, economic, environmental, social, cultural, and national development of the Iranian Elective Monarchy (Elective Shahanshahi).

G) Determining the legal foundations of the financial, monetary, credit, and customs unit market and the circulation of money, as well as determining the foundations of the pricing policy of economic services, including the banks of the Elective Monarchy (Elcctive Shahanshahi) of Iran.

H) Determining the budget, taxes, and charges of the Elective Monarchy (Elective Shahanshahi) of Iran and the funds of the Planning and Budget Organization of the Elective Monarchy (Elective Shahanshahi) of Iran for regional development.

I) Determining the engineering systems of the Elective Monarchy (Elective Shahanshahi) of Iran, nuclear engineering, materials, transportation, railways, information and communication, and space affairs.

J) Determining the foreign policy and international relations of the Elective Monarchy (Elective Shahanshahi) of Iran and Iran's international treaties in cases of war and peace.

K) Determining Iran's foreign economic relations.

L) Determining defense and security policies; purchase and sale of arms, ammunition, and military equipment; and the production of nuclear materials, toxic materials, narcotics, and the method of their utilization.

M) Determining the structure of the judiciary, law enforcement, criminal laws of amnesty and pardon, civil laws, civil procedures and arbitration proceedings, and regulation of intellectual property rights.

N) Settling the conflict between the Elective Monarchy (Elective Shahanshahi) law of Iran and the interpretation of the law.

O) Determining and supervising the meteorological service, norms, models, measurement systems, time measurement, geology, cartography, geographical areas' names, statistics, and official evaluations.

P) Determining and issuing governmental emblems and honorary degrees of Iran's Elective Monarchy (Elective Shahanshahi).

Q) Overseeing the governmental services of the Elected Monarchy (Elective Shahanshahi) of Iran.

Article 106:

1) The joint authorities of the Elective Monarchy (Elective Shahanshahi) of Iran and its subordinate governmental institutions are:

A) Supervising the conformity of the Constitution and other civil laws and the laws of local governments with the Constitution of the Elective Monarchy (Elective Shahanshahi) of Iran and international laws.

B) Protecting the rights and liberties of humans and citizens and promoting the social and cultural rights of Iran's ethnic minorities and the social order and security and rules of the border zones.

C) Determining the ownership, utilization, and exploitation of land, mineral resources, water, and other natural resources.

D) Determining government property.

E) Administering natural resources, environmental protection, and biosecurity, in particular the preservation of natural reserves, and the protection and preservation of historical and cultural staffs.

F) Overseeing general affairs, education, science, culture, physical education, and sports.

G) Coordinating health affairs, preservation of family rights, maternity, paternity, children's rights, and social assistance, including social security.

H) Providing measures to deal with disasters and natural catastrophes and the spread of diseases and to reduce their effects.

I) Determining administrative regulations and procedures, family employment, housing, land, water, forest, natural resources, and environmental preservation regulations.

J) Promoting the public environment and traditional lifestyles of small Iranian ethnic communities.

K) Coordinating and supervising the foreign international relations of provinces and local governments and their adherence to international treaties and the Constitution of the Elective Monarchy (Elective Shahanshahi) of Iran.

2) The provisions of this article shall be applied equally and equitably to all Iranian provinces and local governments.

Article 107:

1) No customs borders, tariffs, duties, or other barriers to the free flow of goods, services, and capital may be established in the territory of the Elective Monarchy (Elective Shahanshahi) of Iran.

2) If it becomes essential to protect people's security, life and health, the environment, and cultural values, limitations on the flow of goods and services shall be imposed by law.

Article 108:

1) The currency of the Elective Monarchy (Elective Shahanshahi) of Iran is the Derik. The issue of currency is the exclusive responsibility of the Central Bank of the Elective Monarchy (Elective Shahanshahi) of Iran. It is not permitted to issue other currencies in the Elective Monarchy (Elective Shahanshahi) of Iran.

2) Supporting and stabilizing the Derik[1] is one of the primary duties of the Central Bank of the Elective Monarchy (Elective

[1] The world's first official gold coin is the "Derik" gold coin minted by command of Dara or Darius, the great Achaemenid Emperor (elected Shahanshah) in the ancient Iranian Empire (Shahanshahi). In 3751. Zoroastrian equals 7751 Aryan-Mithraic, and 2013 AD, large-scale coins of 50 Derik consisting of 300 grams of silver plated with 8 grams of gold were minted by the Afshar Naderi family in remembrance of the great Achaemenid princes and with the titles of Afshar and Achaemenid princes.

Shahanshahi) of Iran, which it performs autonomously from governmental organizations.

3) Iran's tax system, budget, general policies of taxation, and tasks of the Elective Monarchy (Elective Shahanshahi) are determined by domestic laws.

4) Government bonds shall be issued under procedures determined by domestic laws and shall be offered in a fully voluntary manner.

Article 109:

1) In matters related to the authorities of the Elective Monarchy (Elective Shahanshahi) of Iran, under the Constitution and national laws, laws with direct validity shall be enacted throughout the territory of the Elective Monarchy (Elective Shahanshahi) of Iran.

2) In matters related to the common authorities of the Elective Monarchy (Elective Shahanshahi) of Iran and the local governments of the provinces, domestic legislation and, pursuant to these laws, other legal documents of the local governments of the provinces shall be passed.

3) National and local regulations must not be contradictory to the constitutional law of the Elective Monarchy (Elective Shahanshahi) of Iran.

4) Apart from the boundaries of the Elective Monarchy (Elective Shahanshahi) of Iran authorities, and common authorities of the central government and the local governments of the provinces, local governments are in charge of the independent enactment of legal provisions, including the enactment of laws and legal documents.

5) The laws and other legal documents passed in the local governments of the provinces are prohibited from contradicting the national laws and the Constitution of the Elective Monarchy (Elective Shahanshahi) of Iran referred to in the first paragraph of this article. In the event of a conflict between the Constitution or the national law and other legal documents, such as the laws of the local governments of the provinces, the authenticity of the national law and the Constitution shall be confirmed and given priority, and the conflicting local laws shall be automatically nullified.

Article 110:

1) The system and manner of establishment of the organizations of the central government in the local governments of the provinces shall be determined by national law and shall be established independently of the local governments of the provinces.

2) The national organizations and organizations of the executive power of the central government and the executive power of the local governments form the single system of the executive power of the Elective Monarchy (Elective Shahanshahi) Government of Iran within the powers of the central government of the Elective Monarchy (Elective Shahanshahi) Government of Iran and the common authorities of the Elective Monarchy (Elective Shahanshahi) Government of Iran and the local provincial governments.

Article 111:

1) The national organizations of the executive power may establish their own regional and provincial structures to perform their authority and appoint relevant officials.

2) The national organizations of the executive power may delegate part of their powers to the executive bodies of the Elective Monarchy (Elective Shahanshahi) of Iran and the executive bodies of the provincial local governments, based on the agreement between them and the executive bodies of the Elective Monarchy (Elective Shahanshahi) of Iran and the executive bodies of the provincial local governments, if this does not contradict the Constitution of the Elective Monarchy (Elective Shahanshahi) of Iran or the laws of the country.

3) The executive organizations of the provincial local governments may delegate a part of their authorities to them upon agreement with the central executive organizations of the government of the Elective Monarchy (Elective Shahanshahi) of Iran.

4) The Elected Emperor (elected Shahanshah) of Iran, who is appointed for a limited period of seven years, and the Central Government of the Elective Monarchy (Elective Shahanshahi) of Iran, based on the Constitution of Iran, exert the authority and power of the Central Government throughout the territory of the Elective Monarchy (Elective Shahanshahi) of Iran.

Article 112:

The Elective Monarchy (Elective Shahanshahi) of Iran may, under agreements, participate in intergovernmental unions and, in line with international agreements, delegate some of its competencies to them, if this does not violate the rights and liberties of humans, trans-humans, citizens, and trans-citizens; it cannot be opposed to the interests of Iranian civilization, Iranian identity, national interests, and the foundations of the legal system of the Elective Monarchy (Elective Shahanshahi) of Iran.

Chapter 6- Emperor (elected Shahanshah) of Iran

Article 113:

1) The Elected Emperor (elected Shahanshah) of Iran is the guardian and protector of Iran's existence, national sovereignty, independence, territorial integrity, and Iranian identity.

2) The Elected Emperor (elected Shahanshah) of Iran is the actual leader of the Monarchy Guard and the Intelligence Organization of the Monarchy Guard and the symbolic leader of other armed, security, and intelligence forces.

3) The Elected Emperor (elected Shahanshah) of Iran is the king of all provincial kings of the country in local kingdoms and has the right to depose and appoint them.

4) The Elected Emperor (elected Shahanshah) of Iran nominates provincial kings from among the elders of the same province to the Prime Minister for confirmation, and then he/she himself/herself will authorize the decree of the provincial kings.

5) The Elected Emperor (elected Shahanshah) of Iran is the guarantor of the Constitution of the Chosen Emperor (elected Shahanshah) of Iran and the human rights and liberties of the Iranian citizens.

6) The Elected Emperor (elected Shahanshah) of Iran shall determine the major directions of the government's domestic and foreign policies regarding the Iranian country in compliance with the Iranian Constitution.

7) The Elected Emperor (elected Shahanshah) of Iran shall be the symbolic Commander-in-Chief of the Chosen Monarchy Military Force of Iran.

8) The Elected Emperor (elected Shahanshah) of Iran shall recommend two of the seven judges of the Supreme Court and three of the nine judges of the Constitutional Court to the Iran Zamin Association (two houses of the Iranian Parliament) for confirmation.

9) The Elected Emperor (elected Shahanshah) of Iran will recommend to Mahestan the candidate for the position of Attorney General of the country for appointment and discharge.

10) The declarations of war and peace and the state of emergency, which are proposed by the Prime Minister and accepted by the Iranian Parliament (Iran Zamin Association), must be confirmed by the Elected Emperor (elected Shahanshah) of Iran Zamin.

11) The Elected Emperor (elected Shahanshah) awards national medals and honorable titles, high military ranks, and exceptional high titles of the Elected Emperor (elected Shahanshah) of Iran.

12) The Elected Emperor (elected Shahanshah) is entitled to establish his/her office, symbolically called "Darbar."

13) The Elected Emperor, in the case the existence of Iran, Iranian identity, territorial integrity, or national sovereignty is threatened; the Constitution is at risk of annulment and serious deviation as judged by the Constitutional Court; or there is a danger of military coup and revolution, may declare a state of emergency for a limited and renewable period of one year, dismiss the Prime Minister, dissolve the Government and the House of Representatives, and form a provisional government with the help of the Mahestan until the end of the state of emergency and the next elections.

14) In paragraph 13 of Article 113, the Elected Emperor (elected Shahanshah) can convert the content of Iran's Elective Monarchy (Elective Shahanshahi) from a nature similar to a parliamentary republic to a presidential republic for a limited period in an emergency circumstance.

15) Twice a year, on the day of the commencement of Nowruz and the day of the commencement of Mehregan, the Elected

Emperor (elected Shahanshah) gathers the provincial kings in a council called “Iran Zamin Monarchy Association” to consult with them on matters related to the preservation of Iran’s identity and Iranian values and the interests of Iranian civilization. In this forum, the kings, presidents, and rulers of other countries of the Iranian territories, which are located outside the political borders of Iran, are also invited under the Manifesto of the Iranian School of Thought.

16) The Elected Emperor (elected Shahanshah) of Iran is the authorizer of the decree of the elected Prime Minister of the nation.

Article 114:

1) The Elected Emperor (elected Shahanshah) of Iran is elected for a period of seven years by the representatives of the Mahestan of Iran (Senate) on the basis of public and direct elections and by secret voting.

2) Citizens of the Elective Monarchy (Elective Shahanshahi) of Iran who are of Iranian descent and have an Iranian identity and believe in the existence of Iran, who are over 40 years old, who believe in the Manifesto of the Iranian School of Thought, and

have a high-ranking military can be elected as the Emperor (elected Shahanshah) of Iran for a limited period of seven years.

3) No one can hold the position of the Elected Emperor (elected Shahanshah) of Iran for more than three seven-year terms. The sequence or non-sequence of the course is not concerned with this principle.

4) The position of the Elected Emperor (elected Shahanshah) of Iran is not inherited in any way and is not for life; rather, it is an elected position for a limited period of time.

5) The order of election of the Elected Emperor (elected Shahanshah) of Iran is determined by law.

6) The Elected Emperor (elected Shahanshah) of Iran has judicial immunity both during and after his/her term of office, which means that if he/she is accused and dismissed by the Mahestan of Iran, he/she will not be punished beyond the loss of his/her powers.

7) The Elected Emperor (elected Shahanshah) of Iran assumes his/her powers from the time of taking the oath, and the execution of these powers ends with the taking of the oath by the next Elected Emperor (elected Shahanshah).

8) The powers of the Elected Emperor (elected Shahanshah) of Iran cease when he/she resigns or becomes incapable of performing his/her duties due to illness or early dismissal. In such circumstances, the election of the next Elected Emperor (elected Shahanshah) must be held within three months of the termination of the authority of the previous Elected Emperor (elected Shahanshah).

9) In any case where the Elected Emperor (elected Shahanshah) of Iran is incapable of performing his/her duties, the Head of the Mahestan of Iran (Senate-Assembly) shall temporarily fulfill his/her tasks.

10) The Elected Emperor (elected Shahanshah) of Iran may be deposed by the Mahestan of Iran (Senate) based on the accusation of treason against Iran or other serious crimes, which have been confirmed by the Constitutional Court and the Supreme Court on the basis of evidence.

11) The decision of Iran Zamin Mahestan, regarding the filing of charges for the deposition of the Elected Emperor (elected Shahanshah) of Iran, must be made with the majority of 3/4 of the votes of the representatives of Mahestan and according to the opinion of the Special Commission of Mahestan of Iran.

12) The decision of the Iran Zamin Mahestan regarding the dismissal of the Elected Emperor (elected Shahanshah) of Iran must be made within three months after the presentation of the accusations against him/her by the Iran Zamin Mahestan and with a majority of 4/5 of the representatives of Mahestan. If no decision is made within this period, the charges against the Elected Emperor (elected Shahanshah) of Iran shall be dismissed.

Article 115:

1) The Elected Emperor (elected Shahanshah) of Iran administers this swearing in his/her oath of office ceremony:

Almighty, god of souls and knowledge, I pray, in front of the people and their representatives, I swear by the goodness of God of life and wisdom, time and earth, the universe, the sun, the moon, and the souls of the ancestors, founders, and guardians of Iran and the entirety of Iran; in performing my duties as the Elected Emperor (elected Shahanshah) of Iran, I will uphold and support the human and Iranian rights and liberties of Iranians and citizens of Iran; consider and support the Constitution of the Elective Monarchy (Elective Shahanshahi) of Iran; take care of Iran's unity, Iranian identity, independence and security, the country's completeness, and its territorial integrity and national sovereignty; and sincerely be the reason for the unity of the Iranian people and the protector of Iranian interests and Iranian identity in the great Zamin of Iran.

2) The oath of office ceremony will be held at the royal palace with the recitation of the Mehr Yasht Avesta by the Highest Mobad and at the Tomb of Great Ferdowsi in the presence of the representatives of the Iranian Imperial Society, i.e., the representatives of the two Parliaments (Mahestan and House of Representatives), the judges of the Constitutional Court of the Elective Monarchy (Elective Shahanshahi) of Iran, the members of the governmental delegation and the Prime Minister and the provincial kings, the Chief of General Staff of the Armed Forces of the Elective Monarchy (Elective Shahanshahi) of Iran, the Commander of the Army, the Commander of the Monarchy Guard, the Head of the Intelligence Organization of the Monarchy Guard, and the Head of the Country's Intelligence Organization.

3) When the Elected Emperor (elected Shahanshah) takes the Monarchy Oath, he/she wears a royal crown on his/her head, a royal robe on his/her body, and a long scepter and jewels in his/her hand.

4) During his/her swearing-in ceremony, the Elected Emperor (elected Shahanshah) has the authority to use the ancient Mehr rite only symbolically and as a sign of respect for Iran's oldest national

and historic traditions. It should be highlighted that after the swearing-in process, he/she must conduct himself/herself according to Iranian laicity and keep all religious and ritual practices completely separate from his/her duties.

Chapter 7- Parliament of Iran or Iran Zamin Association (Senate and House of Representatives)

Article 116:

The Parliament of Iran is the supreme representative and legislative body of the Elective Monarchy (Elective Shahanshahi) of Iran, which legislates in accordance with strict Iranian laicism, as outlined in the Manifesto of the Iranian School of Thought, and the absolute separation of religion and any other belief from the legislature, according to natural law.

Article 117:

1) The Iranian Parliament consists of two chambers: The Mahestan of Iran and the House of Representatives of Iran.

2) Three representatives from each provincial kingdom (provincial local government) of Iran become members of the Iran Zamin Mahestan (Senate): one from the Provincial Assembly, one from the local government of the province, and one from the elders, prominent, and self-reliant individuals of that province.

3) The House of Representatives of Iran is composed of 777 members.

Article 118:

1) The representatives of the Iran Zamin Association (Parliament of Iran) are appointed for a period of seven years.

2) Arrangements for the establishment of the Iran Zamin Association (Parliament of Iran) and the procedure for choosing its members in Mahestan and the House of Representatives are stipulated by national laws.

Article 119:

1) All citizens of the Elective Monarchy (Elective Shahanshahi) of Iran who have attained the age of 21 years have the right to participate in the elections and can be elected as representatives in the House of Representatives of the country.

2) Only citizens who possess all of the following qualifications can participate in the elections of the Mahestan of Iran:

A) Aged 21 or older.

B) Be Iranian and of Iranian origin.

C) Have an Iranian identity according to the Manifesto of the Iranian School of Thought.

D) Have rendered outstanding services to Iran and Iranians in the scientific, cultural, artistic, social, sporting, political, and economic spheres.

E) Have a civilizational vision, in accordance with the Manifesto of the Iranian School of Thought.

F) Be a believer in the existence of Iran, the historical and essential authenticity of Iran, and Iranian civilization.

3) One person can be the representative of Iran Zamin Mahestan and Iran House of Representatives simultaneously. Representatives of the House of Representatives are not allowed to be members of other bodies representing the state power or local self-governing bodies.

4) The deputies in the House of Representatives of Iran will work on a professional and full-time basis and will not be allowed to engage in social services or any other income-generating activities other than educational, research, and creative activities.

Article 120:

Representatives in the Iranian Parliament shall enjoy immunity during their term of office. The representatives cannot be imprisoned and arrested.

Article 121:

1) The Iran Zamin Association (Parliament of Iran) is a permanent institution.

2) The House of Representatives of Iran holds its first session 30 days after the election.

3) The opening of the first session of the House of Representatives of Iran shall be by the oldest representative.

4) After the commencement of the work of the new House of Representatives, the power of the previous House of Representatives ends.

Article 122:

1) Iran Zamin Mahestan and the House of Representatives of Iran hold sessions separately.

2) The sessions of the representatives of Iran Zamin Mahestan and the House of Iran shall be held in public, and each of them may hold closed sessions in the cases provided for.

3) The two Parliaments may hold a joint session to listen to the messages of the Elected Emperor (elected Shahanshah) of Iran, the messages of the Constitutional Court of Iran, and the speeches of the leaders of foreign countries.

Article 123:

1) Iran Zamin Association (Iranian Parliament) and its two chambers elect their President (elected Shah) and deputies among their representatives.

2) The chairmen of the Mahestan of Iran and the House of Representatives of Iran and their deputies conduct the sessions and set their internal rules.

3) The Mahestan of Iran and the Iranian House of Representatives form committees and commissions and supervise the Iranian Parliament (Iranian Zamin Association) within their powers and hold parliamentary review sessions.

4) Each of the two Parliaments shall have its own set of regulations and shall solve its own problems and organizational issues.

5) Iran Zamin Mahestan and the House of Representatives of Iran form an accounting room to control the country's budget. Its membership and rules of operation are determined by the country's law.

Article 124:

1) The powers of the Mahestan of Iran are:

A) Approving of border changes between the provinces of the country (provincial kingdoms).

B) Approving the decree of the Elected Emperor (elected Shahanshah) of Iran regarding the imposition of martial law.

C) Approving the decree of the Elected Emperor (elected Shahanshah) of Iran to declare a state of emergency.

D) To call for holding parliamentary elections.

E) Election and dismissal of the Elected Emperor (elected Shahanshah) of Iran.

F) Appointing the judges of the Selective Imperial Constitutional Court of Iran and the Supreme Court after the approval of the House of Representatives.

G) Appointing and dismissing of the head and half of the members of the Chamber of Accounts.

H) Approving of national laws approved by the House of Representatives of Iran.

I) Proposing three out of seven judges of the Supreme Court and four out of nine judges of the Constitutional Court to the Iranian Parliament.

Article 125:

1) Iran Zamin Mahestan issues approvals within its powers.

2) Decrees of the Iran Zamin Mahestan shall be subject to the approval of the majority of its representatives.

Article 126:

1) The competencies of the House of Representatives of Iran are as follows:

A) Electing the Prime Minister of the country from the party with the highest number of votes in the national elections.

B) Deciding on the vote of confidence in the government proposed by the elected Prime Minister.

C) Appointing and dismissing the governor of the Central Bank of the Elective Monarchy (Elective Shahanshahi) of Iran.

D) Installing and dismissing the head of the Chamber of Accounts and half of its members.

E) Installing and dismissing the Plenipotentiary for Human Rights under the Constitution of the country.

F) Declaring amnesty.

G) Presenting charges against the Elected Emperor (elected Shahanshah) of Iran for his/her deposition by the Mahestan of Iran.

H) Approving governmental bills and national legislation.

Article 127:

1) In accordance with the Constitution and its powers, the House of Representatives of Iran shall issue its approvals.

2) The majority of its members must agree to the approvals of the Iranian House of Representatives.

Article 128:

1) The President (elected Shah) of the Mahestan of Iran, the House of Representatives of Iran, the representatives of the Mahestan and the House of Representatives, the Elective Monarchy (Elective Shahanshahi) Government of Iran, and legislative bodies such as the Constitutional Court of Iran are entitled to prepare and recommend laws.

2) The bills are submitted to the House of Representatives of Iran.

3) Bills concerning the establishment or abolition of taxes and exemptions from their payment, government loans, changes in the government's financial obligations, and other bills related to the government's budget expenditures are submitted to the House of Representatives of Iran only with the government's approval.

4) The Elective Monarchy (Elective Shahanshahi) country of Iran is a laic country based on the Iranian laicism in the Manifesto of the Iranian School of Thought. In the interest of respect and freedom for all religions and their followers, no religious law or law inspired by religion will have the right to be proposed and approved in the two Parliaments of Iran.

Article 129:

1) National laws are approved in the House of Representatives of Iran.

2) National laws must be approved by the majority of the members of the House of Representatives of Iran unless the Constitution stipulates otherwise.

3) The laws approved in the House of Representatives of Iran will be given to Iran Zamin Mahestan within seven days.

4) If within 14 days after the submission of a national law to the Iran Zamin Mahestan, this body does not express its opinion or is approved by the majority of Mahestan's representatives, this law will be considered as approved by the Iran Zamin Association (Parliament of Iran). If the Iran Zamin Mahestan rejects the law of the country, the two Parliaments can form an understanding commission to resolve the differences, then the said law will be returned to the House of Representatives of Iran for review.

5) If the House of Representatives of Iran does not agree with the decision of the Iran Zamin Mahestan, if the national law is approved by 3/4 of the representatives of the House of Representatives in the revote, it shall be considered approved.

Article 130:

The laws of the country, which have been approved in the House of Representatives of Iran, if they are in the following fields, are examined in the specialized commissions of Mahestan, Iran, before approval:

1) National budget

2) Governmental taxes and duties

3) Financial, monetary, credit, customs, and currency circulation regulations

4) Approval and cancellation of the international contract of the Elected Monarchy (Elective Shahanshahi) of Iran

5) The state and protection of the state borders of the government of the Elective Monarchy (Elective Shahanshahi) of Iran

6) War and peace

Article 131:

1) The approved Constitution of the Elective Monarchy (Elective Shahanshahi) of Iran and any amendments to it will be sent to the Elected Emperor (elected Shahanshah) of Iran for signature and promulgation within seven days.

2) The Chosen Emperor (elected Shahanshah) of Iran has the right to veto the laws of the Iran Zamin Association of the Iranian Parliament if they conflict with the interests of Iran's national pride, Iranian identity, national sovereignty, and territorial integrity of Iran.

3) The Elected Emperor (elected Shahanshah) of Iran shall not have the right to veto his/her dismissal in the Mahestan of Iran if it is approved by 4/5 of the representatives of the Mahestan.

Article 132:

1) The Elected Emperor (elected Shahanshah) of Iran may dissolve the House of Representatives of Iran himself/herself or on the proposal of the Prime Minister if it is necessary in the interests of the honor of Iran, national sovereignty, and the preservation of the territorial integrity of Iran.

2) In case of dissolution of the House of Representatives of Iran, the Elected Emperor (elected Shahanshah) shall set the date of the new national elections in such a way that the new Parliament convenes within seven months after the dissolution of the former Parliament.

3) The House of Representatives of Iran cannot be dissolved from the time of the presentation of the charges against the Elected Emperor (elected Shahanshah) until the decision of the Mahestan of Iran on the matter.

4) The House of Representatives of Iran cannot be dissolved during a state of emergency or martial law in the entire territory of the Elective Monarchy (Elective Shahanshahi) of Iran, as well as six months until the end of the reign of the Elected Emperor (elected Shahanshah).

5) Iran Zamin Mahestan cannot be dissolved under any conditions and by anyone. Only after seven years from the beginning of each term should it be reconstituted through national elections.

Chapter 8- The Prime Ministry and the Elected Monarchy (Elective Shahanshahi) Government of Iran

Article 133:

Elected Prime Minister of Iran:

1): The Prime Minister is the head of the Elected Monarchy (Elective Shahanshahi) Government of Iran. The Prime Minister is chosen from the party that won the most votes in the country's parliamentary elections and is appointed to form the government based on strict Iranian laicism as outlined in the Manifesto of the Iranian School of Thought.

2) The Prime Minister is appointed to form the government on the proposal of his/her party and the Speaker of the House of Representatives of Iran, and after the vote of confidence of the two Parliaments of Iran on the members of his/her cabinet, his/her decision must be implemented by the Elected Emperor (elected Shahanshah) of Iran.

3) The Prime Minister decides on the resignation of the Elective Monarchy (Elective Shahanshahi) Government of Iran.

4) The Prime Minister presents the candidate for the Central Bank of Iran to the Parliament of Iran (Iran Zamin Association).

5) The Prime Minister submits the proposal for the dismissal of the head of the Central Bank of Iran to the Iranian Parliament

6) The Prime Minister is in charge of dismissing and appointing his/her deputies and advisors.

7) The Prime Minister has the following responsibilities: Nominating two candidates out of nine judges of the Constitutional Court; two judges out of seven judges of the Supreme Court; the Prosecutor General of the country to the Iranian Parliament for approval; and appointment, proposing, the dismissal of the Prosecutor General of the country to the Iranian Parliament.

8) The formation and leadership of the National Security Council of the Iranian Monarchy is optional with the Prime Minister.

9) The Prime Minister is responsible for approving the regulations of the mandatory service of the Iranian monarchy.

10) The Prime Minister is responsible for creating the office of the Elective Monarchy (Elective Shahanshahi) Prime Minister of Iran.

11) The Prime Minister is responsible for the dismissal and appointment of his/her plenipotentiaries.

12) The Prime Minister is responsible for the dismissal and appointment of the Commanders-in-Chief of the Armed Forces of

the Elective Monarchy (Elective Shahanshahi) of Iran, with the exception of the Commanders-in-Chief of the Iranian Monarchy Guard.

13) The Prime Minister is in charge of dismissing and appointing Iran's diplomatic representatives in foreign countries and international organizations after consultation with the relevant commissions or committees of the Iranian Parliament (Iran Zamin Association).

14) The Prime Minister is responsible for holding the elections to the Iran Zamin Association (the two houses of the Iranian Parliament) in accordance with the Constitution and the laws of the country.

15) It is the responsibility of the Prime Minister to hold a referendum in the order specified in the Constitution.

16) It is the responsibility of the Prime Minister to submit bills to the Iranian Parliament.

17) It is the responsibility of the Prime Minister to sign and promulgate national laws.

18) It is the responsibility of the Prime Minister to present an annual message to the Iranian Parliament on the state of the

country based on the main orientations of the country's domestic and foreign policies.

19) The nomination of the head of the country's intelligence organization, except the head of the intelligence organization of the Iranian Territorial Monarchy Guard, to the Iranian Parliament (Iranian Territorial Association) is the responsibility of the Prime Minister.

20) The proposal of provincial kingdoms by the Elected Emperor (elected Shahanshah) for removal and installation is done with the approval of the Prime Minister and the implementation of the Elected Emperor (elected Shahanshah).

Article 134:

1) The Prime Minister of Iran can make use of the dispute settlement arrangements of the country's governmental bodies. In case of disagreement on any of the decisions, he/she can refer these disputes to the competent court.

2) The Prime Minister of Iran has the right to suspend the validity of the legal documents of the executive bodies of the provincial kingdoms (local governments) if these documents are inconsistent with the Constitution of the Elective Monarchy (Elective Shahanshahi) of Iran and the national laws and international

obligations of the country or the rights and freedoms of humans, trans-humans, citizens, and trans-citizens violate the pride of Iran, Iranian national identity, national sovereignty and territorial integrity of the country; in this case, the Prime Minister may refer the violation to the Constitutional Court.

Article 135:

The elected Prime Minister of Iran shall:

1) Supervise and direct the foreign policy of the country.

2) Be responsible for conducting negotiations and signing international treaties of the Iranian Elective Monarchy (Elective Shahanshahi).

3) Be responsible for signing agreements.

4) Receive letters of credence from diplomatic representatives.

Article 136:

1) The Elected Monarchy (Elective Shahanshahi) Prime Minister of Iran is the Commander-in-Chief of the country's armed, security, and intelligence forces, with the exception of the Monarchy Guard and the Monarchy Guard Intelligence Organization. The symbolic Commander-in-Chief of all forces is

under the responsibility of the Elected Emperor (elected Shahanshah) of Iran.

2) In case of an attack on the Elected Monarchy (Elective Shahanshahi) of Iran or an imminent threat to it, the Prime Minister shall propose to the Parliament of Iran (Iran Zamin Association) the declaration of a state of emergency, a state of war, and martial law and its regulations throughout the country or in its regions, and if approved by the legislature and approved by the Elected Emperor (elected Shahanshah) of Iran, he/she may implement his/her proposal.

3) The Prime Minister's proposal to the Iranian Parliament and the chosen Emperor (elected Shahanshah) to declare a state of emergency, a state of war, and martial law and its arrangements must be for a limited period of not more than one year, and if necessary, it can be extended annually after the approval of the Parliament and the approval of the chosen Emperor (elected Shahanshah).

Article 137:

1) The Prime Minister of the Elective Monarchy (Elective Shahanshahi) of Iran issues decrees and executive orders.

2) The decrees and orders of the Prime Minister of the Elective Monarchy (Elective Shahanshahi) of Iran must be implemented throughout the territory of Iran and have executory sanctions.

3) The decrees and orders of the Prime Minister must not be in contradiction with the Constitution of the country and the national laws.

Article 138:

The Prime Minister of Iran has judicial immunity during his/her term of office.

Article 139:

1) The elected Prime Minister of Iran assumes his/her powers and responsibilities from the time of taking the oath, and the exercise of these powers ends when the new Prime Minister of the country takes the oath.

2) The powers of the elected Prime Minister of the Iranian Monarchy end when he/she resigns or is unable to perform his/her duties due to illness or early dismissal. In such a situation, the party that has the most seats in the Iranian Parliament (Iran Zamin

Association) must present the new Prime Minister to the Parliament and the Elected Emperor (elected Shahanshah).

3) In all cases when the Prime Minister is unable to perform his/her duties, the Speaker of the House of Representatives temporarily performs his/her duties. The guarantor of Iran's Elective Monarchy (Elective Shahanshahi), the Prime Minister, does not have the right to dissolve government institutions, hold referendums, and propose amendments to the articles of the country's Constitution.

Article 140:

1) The Prime Minister of the Iranian Elective Monarchy (Elective Shahanshahi) can be removed on the basis of an accusation by the Iranian Parliament (two houses of the Iran Zamin Association) of treason or other serious crimes and approval by the Constitutional Court or the Supreme Court by the Iranian Parliament (two houses of the Iran Zamin Association).

2) The decision of the Iran Zamin Association (two houses of the Iranian Parliament) to dismiss the Prime Minister after the approval of the Constitutional Court or the Supreme Court must be taken by the majority of the representatives of each of the two

houses and based on the opinion of the Special Commission of the Iran Zamin Association (Parliament of Iran).

3) The decision of the Iran Zamin Association (the two houses of the Iranian Parliament) on the dismissal of the Prime Minister must be made within three months after the charges against him/her are presented by the majority of the two houses of the country's Parliament; if no decision is made within this period, the charges against the Prime Minister are automatically dropped.

4) The Prime Minister may be dismissed by his/her own internal party mechanism.

Article 141:

1) The Elective Monarchical Government of Iran exercises executive power throughout the country.

2) The Elective Monarchy (Elective Shahanshahi) Government of Iran consists of the Prime Minister, his/her deputies, and the ministers of the ministries.

Article 142:

1) The Prime Minister of the Elective Monarchy (Elective Shahanshahi) Government of Iran is appointed by the winning party in the national elections or the party that has received the maximum number of popular votes with the approval of the Iran

Zamin Association (two houses of the Iranian Parliament), and his/her Prime Ministerial Decree is enforced by the Elected Emperor (elected Shahanshah).

2) The proposal of the new Prime Minister of the elected imperial government of Iran less than two weeks after the beginning of the new House of Representatives or after the resignation of the previous government, or within one week after the rejection of the prime ministerial candidate by the Iranian Zamin Association (Parliament of Iran), the party with the most seats in the House of Representatives must be presented.

3) The country's Parliament must examine the candidate for Prime Minister within one week after the nomination of the party with the most seats in the House of Representatives.

4) After both houses of the country's Parliament have rejected the candidate for Prime Minister proposed by the majority party three times, the House of Representatives is dissolved and new elections are held.

Article 143:

1) In less than one week after the execution of his/her decree by the Elected Emperor (elected Shahanshah), the Prime Minister of Iran's Elective Monarchy (Elective Shahanshahi) submits his/her

proposal regarding the structure of the executive branch and the ministers of the ministries to the two houses of the Iranian Parliament and appoints his/her deputies and advisors.

2) The activities of the government of the Iranian Elective Monarchy (Elective Shahanshahi) are regulated by the Constitution of the Iranian Elective Monarchy (Elective Shahanshahi).

Article 144:

In accordance with the interests of Iran's identity, the country's Constitution and laws, and Iran's strict laicism as stipulated in the Manifesto of the Iranian School of Thought, the elected monarchical Prime Minister of Iran will be responsible for leading and presiding over the government of Iran and regulating its activities.

Article 145:

1) The Prime Minister prepares the annual budget of the country and submits it to the two Houses of the Parliament of the country (Iran Zamin Association) for approval, undertakes its implementation, and submits a report on its implementation to the two Houses of the Parliament of the country.

2) The Prime Minister is responsible for financial, credit, and monetary policies in the Elective Monarchy (Elective Shahanshahi) country of Iran.

3) The Prime Minister is responsible for ensuring the rule of law, the rights and freedoms of citizens, the protection of property and public order, and the control of crime.

4) The Prime Minister shall exercise all other powers vested in him/her by the Constitution of the Elective Monarchy (Elective Shahanshahi) of Iran and the laws of the country.

Article 146:

1) The government of the Elective Monarchy (Elective Shahanshahi) of Iran will issue and implement orders and decrees based on the Constitution of the country and national laws.

2) The orders and decrees of the Elective Monarchy (Elective Shahanshahi) Government of Iran must be implemented and sanctioned throughout the country.

3) The orders and decrees of the Elective Monarchy (Elective Shahanshahi) Government of Iran, if they conflict with the Constitution and national laws, the Supreme Court and the Constitutional Court can cancel them.

Article 147:

The Elective Monarchy (Elective Shahanshahi) Government of Iran shall hand over its power to the new government after the expiration of its term and the holding of new elections.

Article 148:

1) The Elective Monarchy (Elective Shahanshahi) Government of Iran may resign.

2) The Prime Minister of the Elective Monarchy (Elective Shahanshahi) of Iran may decide to dismiss the government.

3) The two houses of the Iranian Parliament (Iran Zamin Association) may vote no confidence in the government. The vote of no confidence is passed by the majority of the votes of the representatives. If the Parliament of the country announces its vote of no confidence in the government again within three months, the Prime Minister can dismiss the government and propose a new government or dissolve the House of Representatives and announce early elections.

4) The Prime Minister of Iran can request a vote of confidence in the government from both houses of the country's Parliament. If the Parliament of the country passes a vote of no confidence, the

Prime Minister can decide within seven days to dismiss the government or dissolve the House of Representatives and hold new elections.

5) If the Elective Monarchy (Elective Shahanshahi) Government of Iran resigns or refuses to exercise its powers, it must continue to work under the leadership of the President (elected Shah) of the Senate until the new government of the country is formed.

Chapter 9- Judiciary

Article 149:

1) Judging in Iran's Elective Monarchy (Elective Shahanshahi) is done only by lay courts with the strict characteristics of Iranian laicity and the complete separation of religion and any ritual from judgment.

2) The judicial system in Iran has the following five levels:

A) Constitutional Court

B) Supreme Court of the country

C) National Courts

D) Provincial Courts

E) Urban Courts

3) The head and supervision of the entire judicial system of Iran lies with the President (elected Shah) of the Constitutional Court of the Iranian Monarchy.

4) The judiciary performs its duty according to the Constitution, civil law, and laïque criminal law.

5) The judicial system of the Iranian monarchy is established by the Constitution of the country. The establishment of special

courts is forbidden except in the intelligence and security organizations of the country.

Article 150:

Citizens of Iran's Elective Monarchy (Elective Shahanshahi) who are over 33 years old, have legal education, and at least five years of legal work experience can become judges. Additional conditions for judging in the country's courts may be determined by the Citizenship Law.

Article 151:

1) Judgment is independent and subject only to the Constitution of the Elective Monarchy (Elective Shahanshahi) of Iran and the laws of citizenship and criminal law.

2) If any governmental document or other institution is found to be inconsistent with the law, a verdict will be issued according to the law.

Article 152:

1) The judge cannot be changed.

2) The authority of the judge shall not be terminated or suspended except in accordance with the provisions of the Law on Citizenship and Trans-Citizenship.

Article 153:

1) Judges have immunity.

2) A judge may be prosecuted only under the conditions specified in the Law on Citizenship and Trans-Citizenship.

Article 154:

1) All trials shall be held in open courts. In the cases determined by the Law on Citizenship and Trans-Citizenship, a closed session may be held.

2) Criminal cases shall not be examined without the presence of the accused, except in the cases stipulated by the Law on Citizenship and Trans-Citizenship.

3) The trial shall be conducted based on the procedure based on the dispute and the equality of the litigants.

4) In the cases specified in the Law on Citizenship and Trans-Citizenship, the trial shall be held in the presence of a jury.

Article 155:

The expenses of the judicial courts shall be financed only from the state budget, and this is so that the independent administration of the courts is following the Law of Citizenship and Trans-Citizenship.

Article 156:

1) The Elective Monarchy (Elective Shahanshahi) Constitutional Court of Iran is the highest judicial authority of the country, focusing on disputes and compliance with the Constitution, and consists of nine judges.

2) The Constitutional Court of the Elective Monarchy (Elective Shahanshahi) of Iran shall determine the conformity of the following with the Constitution:

A) Citizenship and extra-citizenship laws, executive regulations of the Prime Minister, Mahestan, the House of Representatives, and the government of the Elective Monarchy (Elective Shahanshahi) of Iran.

B) Citizenship and extra-citizenship laws of provincial assemblies and executive regulations of provincial kingdoms and local governments and rulings of provincial courts and other national and urban courts and even rulings of the Supreme Court in terms of compliance with the Constitution.

C) Agreements between various institutions of executive power in Iran's Elective Monarchy (Elective Shahanshahi) and institutions of executive power in provincial kingdoms (local governments).

D) The international agreements of Iran's Elective Monarchy (Elective Shahanshahi) that have not been implemented.

3) The Constitutional Court of the Elective Monarchy (Elective Shahanshahi) of Iran shall decide on the following disputes:

A) Disputes between governmental bodies.

B) Disputes between the central government and provincial kingdoms (local governments).

4) The Constitutional Court of the Elective Monarchy (Elective Shahanshahi) of Iran, based on the regulations stipulated in the Citizenship and Trans-Citizenship Law, examines the complaint of a violation of rights and freedoms based on the Constitution and the request of the courts regarding the conformity of the law to be applied in the cases with the Constitution.

5) The Elective Monarchy (Elective Shahanshahi) Constitutional Court of Iran interprets the Constitution upon the request of the Elected Emperor (elected Shahanshah) of Iran, the Prime Minister, the Mahestan, the House of Representatives, and the provincial kingdoms and their governments, assemblies, and local courts.

6) Legal documents and materials from them, which are known to be in contradiction with the Constitution, lose their validity. If the international agreements of the Elected Monarchy (Elective Shahanshahi) of Iran are against the Constitution, they should not be applied and implemented.

7) The Constitutional Court of the Elective Monarchy (Elective Shahanshahi) of Iran, at the request of the 4/5 majority of Mahestan, shall pass judgment on the charges of treason or violation of the Constitution on the part of the Chosen Emperor (elected Shahanshah).

Article 157:

The Supreme Court of the country shall be composed of seven judges and shall be the highest judicial body in matters of citizenship and trans-citizenship, criminal, administrative, and other matters that fall under the general jurisdiction of the courts;

it shall exercise its supervision over these matters in the order determined in the practical procedures of citizenship and trans-citizenship and the laws of the country and shall issue the necessary rulings and explanations regarding legal issues and actions.

Article 158:

1) The judges of the Constitutional Court consist of nine judges: four judges are elected on the proposal of the Head of Mahestan, three judges are elected on the proposal of the Emperor (elected Shahanshah), and two judges are nominated on the proposal of the Prime Minister. Then they are appointed to the position of judges of the Constitutional Court for a period of seven years by the majority vote of the representatives in the Iran Zamin Association (the two houses of the Iranian Parliament).

2) The judges of the Supreme Court include seven judges: three judges were selected by the proposal of the Mahestan, two judges were selected by the proposal of the Monarch, and two other judges were nominated by the proposal of the Prime Minister. After obtaining the majority of votes in the Iran Zamin Association (the two houses of the Iranian Parliament), they are appointed to the Supreme Court.

3) Other judges of the country's courts are appointed on the basis of the regulations stipulated in the country's Citizenship and Trans-Citizenship Laws, and the country's Supreme Court supervises the selection process of judges.

4) The powers of the Constitutional Court, the Supreme Court, and the national, provincial, and municipal courts and their regulations shall be based on the Constitution.

Article 159:

1) The Prosecutor General of the country is a single, centralized system in the Elective Monarchy (Elective Shahanshahi) of Iran, where the lower prosecutors are subordinate to the higher prosecutors and the Prosecutor General of the Elective Monarchy (Elective Shahanshahi) of Iran. The Prosecutor General of the country is chosen on the proposal of the Emperor (elected Shahanshah) and is removed and installed by the Mahestan of Iran.

2) Provincial Prosecutors are appointed by the Prosecutor General of the Iranian Monarchy in accordance with the opinion of the Mahestan of Iran and his/her Senators.

3) Other prosecutors are appointed by the Prosecutor General of the country.

4) The powers of organization and operation of the Public Prosecutor's Office are determined by national and civil laws.

Chapter 10- Provincial Governments (Provincial Kingdoms or Local Governments)

Article 160:

1) Local self-government in the provinces of the united country of the Elective Monarchy (Elective Shahanshahi) of Iran for the independent solution of the problems of the people of the provinces and limited executive, legislative, and judicial management, in accordance with the Constitution and while the three central powers of the country and not in parallel, in the hands of the people themselves.

2) Local self-government shall be exercised by the citizens of the provinces in various forms of local elections to elect the representatives of the provincial Parliament and then the provincial government and the First Minister of the province (the head of the provincial government) from this Parliament, as well as by the urban and rural associations elected by the people.

3) The provincial kings are nominated by the Elected Emperor (elected Shahanshah) from among the elders of that province and are appointed with the approval of the Prime Minister and the execution of their orders by the Elected Emperor (elected Shahanshah) of Iran. Provincial kings are ceremonial officials

with limited responsibilities to protect national unity, Iranian identity, and Iranian pride in the provinces. The provincial kings are the guardians of Iran's identity in the provinces, and only in case of crisis, war, rebellion, and separatism, the provinces are allowed to dissolve the provincial Parliament and government and request the Elected Emperor (elected Shahanshah) to declare a state of emergency and request the Prime Minister of the central government in the province to hold new elections for the provincial Parliament. The Provincial King also proposes provincial and city judges to the Provincial Assembly for approval by a majority vote.

4) The Provincial Assembly shall be the supreme local legislative body of the Province, which shall have the power to enact local legislation in accordance with the Constitution of the Nation and the laws of the country, together with and not in parallel with the Constitution of the Nation. The representatives of this Parliament shall be elected in provincial elections from among the independents of the same province and the local factions of the national parties, whose members must be indigenous. The First Minister or the head of the provincial government and the members of the provincial government are members of this Parliament, and this Parliament has the power to dismiss them. This Parliament also has the power to appoint and dismiss

provincial judges proposed by the Provincial King. This Parliament can also demand his/her dismissal from this position if it does not agree with the proposal of the Elected Emperor (elected Shahanshah) and the Prime Minister regarding the candidate of the provincial king.

5) The supreme executive authority of each province and the head of the provincial government shall be the First Minister of that province, who shall be appointed to this position from among the people of the same province and the provincial faction of the national party that has won the most votes in the local assembly elections, upon the proposal of the local faction of the party and the approval of the Prime Minister of the central government.

6) Provincial and city judges shall be appointed on the proposal of the Provincial King and with the approval of the majority of the Provincial Assembly.

7) Local, provincial, and regional parties are not allowed to operate in the provincial kingdoms of the unitary country of Iran's Elective Monarchy (Elective Shahanshahi). In the provinces, only the provincial factions of the national parties whose members come from the people of the same province are allowed to operate.

8) The activity of local, provincial, and regional military and law enforcement forces is prohibited in the provincial kingdoms of the

unitary country of the Iranian Elective Monarchy (Elective Shahanshahi). In the provinces, there is only the provincial branch of the nationwide military and law enforcement forces.

9) Provinces in the Iranian Elective Monarchy (Elective Shahanshahi) Unitary State do not have national sovereignty, and their local government is equal to local administration and is different from regional government in federal and confederal countries.

10) Provinces in the Iranian Elective Monarchy (Elective Shahanshahi) Unitary State do not have territorial integrity, and their local government is equivalent to local administration and is different from regional government in federal and confederal countries.

11) City councils, whose members are elected by the people of the same city, are responsible for the administration of the city. The mayor of each city shall be elected from among the members of the urban association by a vote within the association.

12) Rural associations, whose members are elected by the people of the same village, are responsible for village management. The Kadkhoda or chief of the village is elected by every 10 members of the rural association by voting within the association.

Article 161:

1) Local self-government in cities, rural areas, and other places will be implemented according to the historical and ethnic, not religious, traditions of the province. Respect for traditions should be such that it does not violate the principles of modernism and strict Iranian laicism as stated in the Manifesto of the Iranian School of Thought.

2) The structure of provincial self-governing bodies and their heads are determined by the people of the province.

3) Changes in the geographical scope of provincial, local self-governments are made with the consent of the indigenous people of the same province, although the provinces do not have territorial integrity in the Elective Monarchy (Elective Shahanshahi) unitary country of Iran.

Article 162:

1) Local self-government bodies manage local property, approve and implement local budgets, impose local taxes and duties, ensure law and order, and resolve other local issues.

2) Local self-government bodies can enjoy some powers of the central government and its facilities and properties by law. The

government shall supervise the transfer of such powers, facilities, and properties.

3) The provincial budget is a part of the national budget, and according to the economic and cultural development index and the population of the province, the Premier of the Central Government refers to the Provincial Assembly for approval and implementation. Obviously, more funds should be allocated for the development of regions whose growth indicators are lower than the national average.

4) Oil wells, gas wells, gold mines, silver mines, diamond mines, uranium mines, and nuclear power plants are the wealth of the entire country of the Monarchical Unitary State of Iran and do not belong to any particular province, but the provincial local government has priority in using other resources located in that province to supplement its budget.

5) The priority of using water resources is with the province in which these resources are located, and only after the needs of water resources in this province have been met can they be used for the rest of the provinces.

Article 163:

1) The duration of the responsibility of the Provincial King is a period of seven years, and each person can be appointed to this position for a maximum of two terms, the sequence or non-sequence of terms has no effect on this principle.

2) The duration of the responsibility of the First Minister of a province is a period of seven years, and each person can be appointed to this position for a maximum of two terms, the sequence or non-sequence of terms has no effect in this principle.

3) The term of responsibility of the Provincial Assembly is a period of seven years, after which provincial elections must be held to form a new assembly.

4) The term of responsibility of the urban associations is a period of seven years, after which the elections of the urban associations must be held to form a new association.

5) The duration of the responsibility of the rural associations is a period of seven years, after which the elections of the rural associations must be held to form a new association.

6) The duration of the responsibility of the mayor is a period of 3.5 years and a maximum of two terms. At the end of the first

term, a vote must be held among the members of the urban association to elect a new mayor.

7) The term of responsibility of the Village Chief is 3.5 years and a maximum of two terms. At the end of the first term, a vote must be held among the members of the rural association to elect a new Village Chief.

Article 164:

Provincial kingdoms and local self-government in Iran's Elective Monarchy (Elective Shahanshahi) Unitary State are guaranteed on the condition that they do not violate the Constitution and are guaranteed during the reign and not parallel to it.

Chapter 11- Constitutional Reforms and Revisions

Article 165:

Proposals for amendments and revisions to the Constitution of the Iranian Elective Monarchy (Elective Shahanshahi) may be submitted by the Elected Emperor (elected Shahanshah) or the Head of the Mahestan.

Article 166:

1) The Constituent Assembly shall be formed by order of the proposer of the amendments (Elected Emperor (elected Shahanshah) or Head of Mahestan) to carry out the amendments to the Constitution.

2) The Constituent Assembly prepares a draft of the new Constitution or amendments to the old one. Such a draft must be approved by 2/3 of the representatives of the Constitutional Assembly.

3) The new Constitution must be approved by 4/5 of the representatives of Mahestan.

4) After approval by the representatives of the Constituent Assembly and the Mahestan, the new Constitution must be

submitted to a referendum and a general vote of the people, and if it is approved by more than half of the voters, it is considered approved.

Article 167:

1) Any amendment to the Constitution that violates national sovereignty, territorial integrity, Iranian identity, and legitimacy, and endangers the pride of Iran and the historical, natural, and cultural continuity of Iran and Iranian civilization is prohibited.

2) In any amendment to the Constitution, the Manifesto of the Iranian School of Thought (Iranian Vesta) should be considered the highest scientific and philosophical reference for the analysis of Iranian history and civilization.

References and Sources

1) Hazeli, Reza (2015). *Manifesto of the Iranzamin School of Thought.* Amazon Publication.

Appendixes

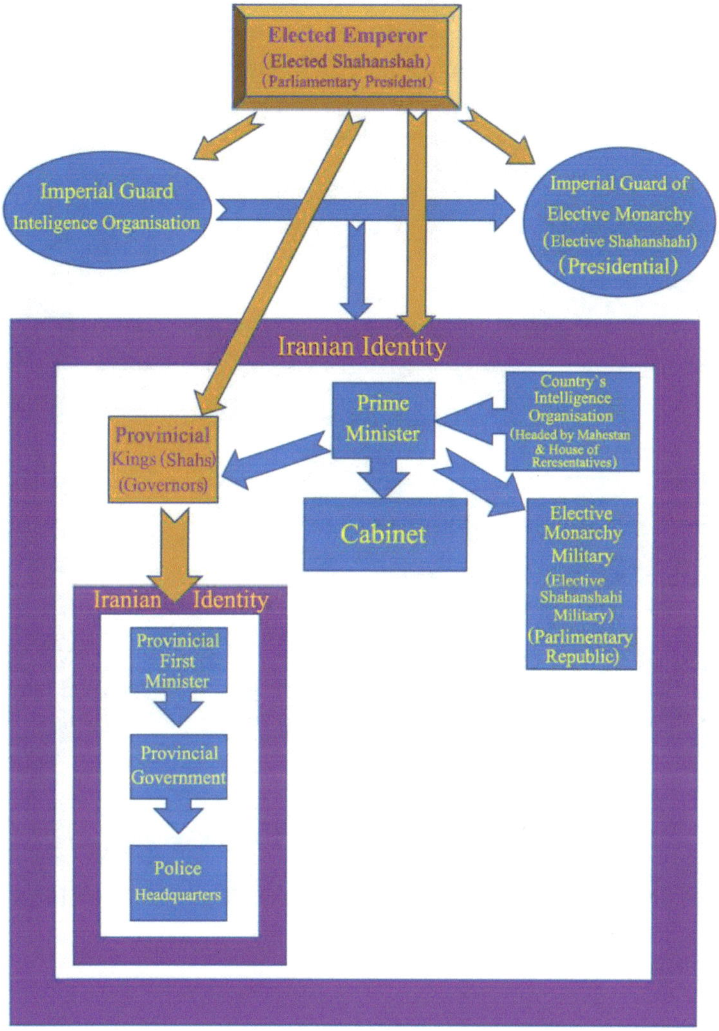
Elected Emperor
(Elected Shahanshah)
(Parliamentary President)
Imperial Guard
Inteligence Organisation
Imperial Guard of
Elective Monarchy
(Elective Shahanshahi)
(Presidential)
Iranian Identity
Prime
Minister
Country`s
Intelligence
Organisation
(Headed by Mahestan
& House of
Reresentatives)
Provinicial
Kings (Shahs)
(Governors)
Cabinet
Elective
Monarchy
Military
(Elective
Shahanshahi
Military)
(Parlimentary
Republic)
Iranian Identity
Provinicial
First
Minister
Provincial
Government
Police
Headquarters

Legislative and Executive Powers and the Role of People in Iran`s Elective Monarchy National Democracy

(Parliamentary Republic with Preservation of Ancient Iranian Political Tradition)

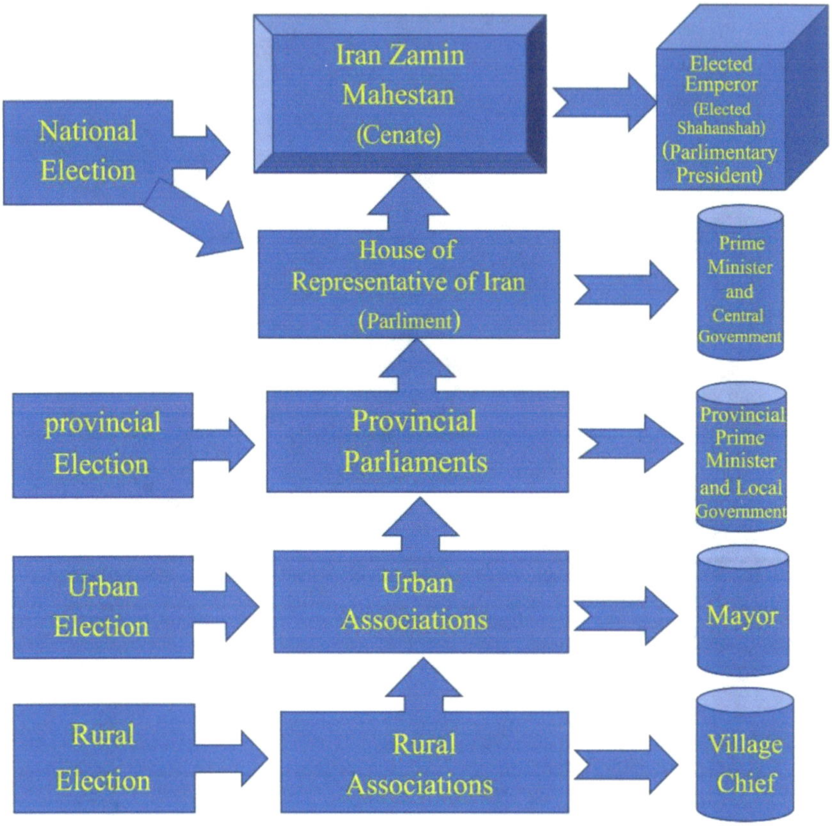

Judiciary and the Process of Appointment of Supreme Court Judges

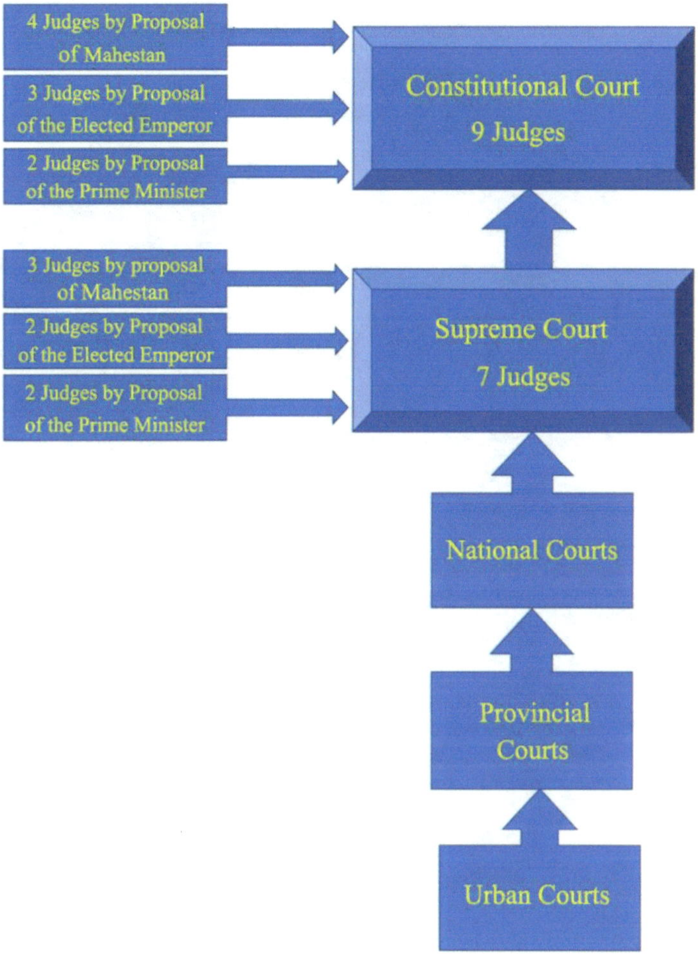

Judiciary According to the Iranzamin School of Thought

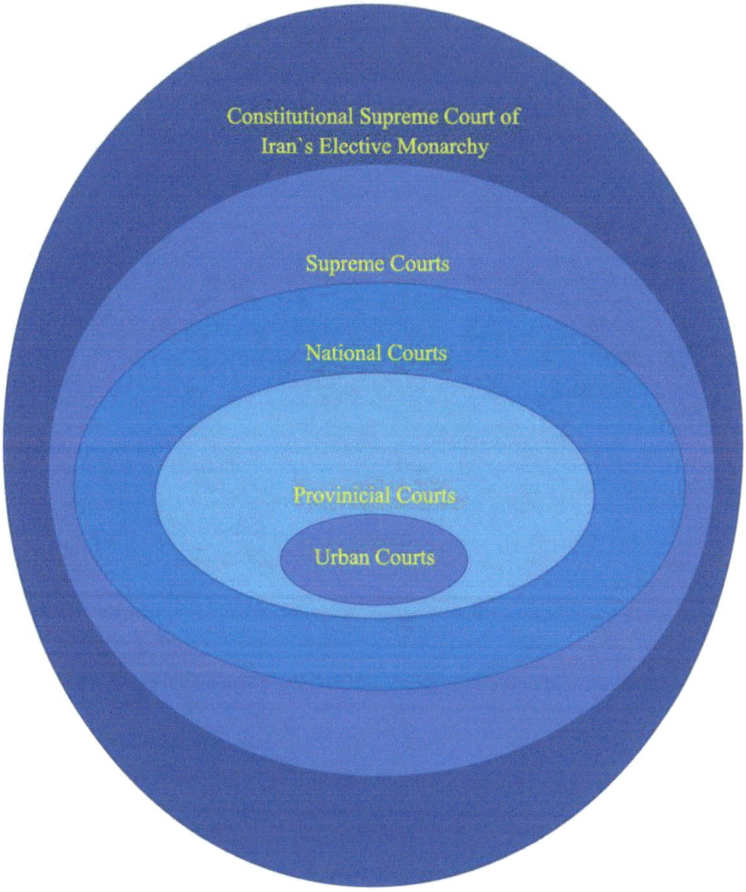

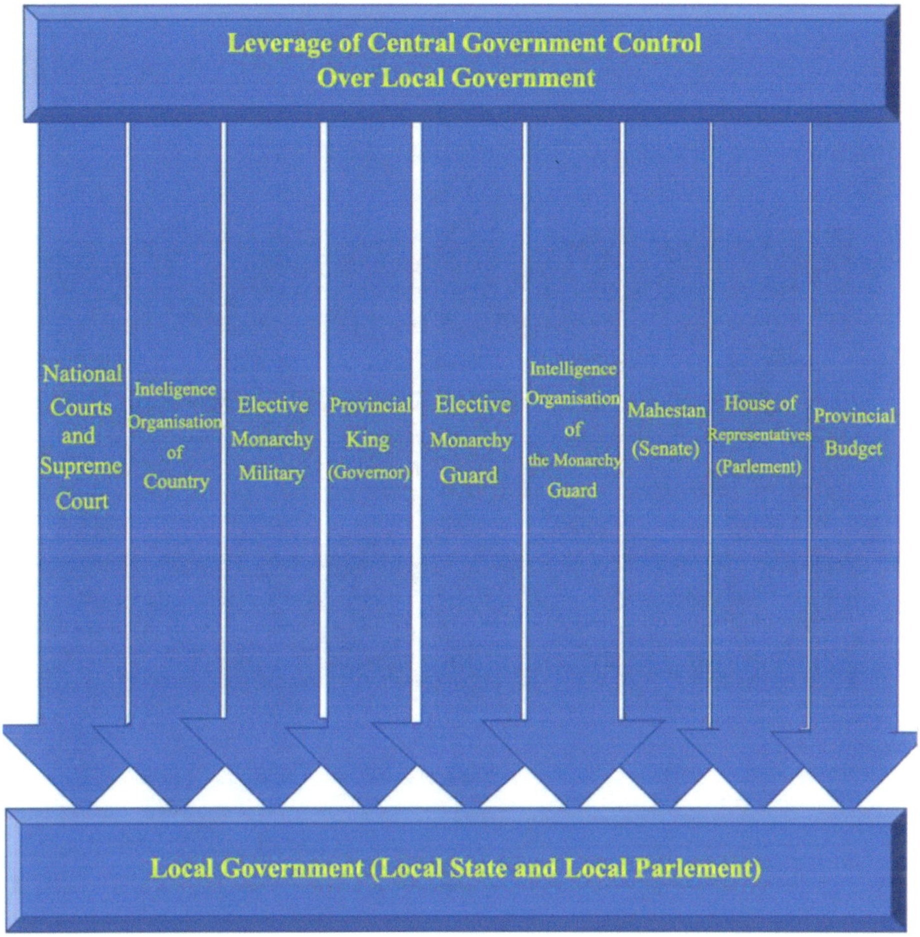
Leverage of Central Government Control
Over Local Government
National Courts and Supreme Court
Inteligence Organisation of Country
Elective Monarchy Military
Provincial King (Governor)
Elective Monarchy Guard
Intelligence Organisation of the Monarchy Guard
Mahestan (Senate)
House of Representatives (Parlement)
Provincial Budget
Local Government (Local State and Local Parlement)

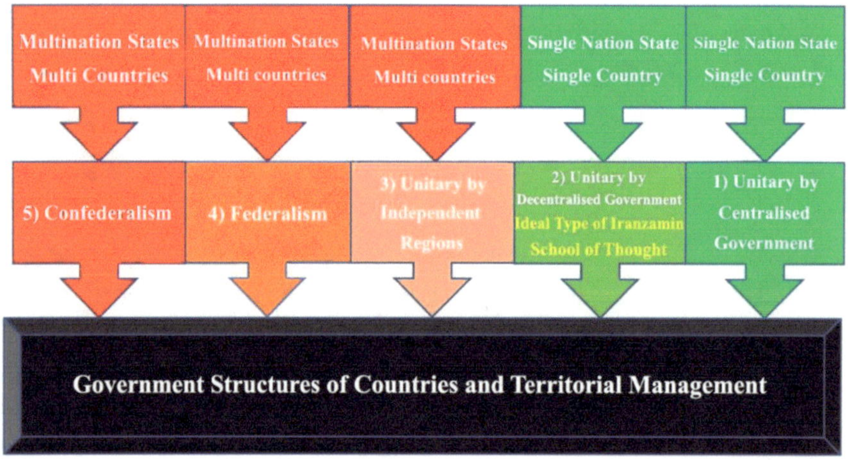
Multination States
Multi Countries
Multination States
Multi countries
Multination States
Multi countries
Single Nation State
Single Country
Single Nation State
Single Country
5) Confederalism
4) Federalism
3) Unitary by
Independent
Regions
2) Unitary by
Decentralised Government
Ideal Type of Iranzamin
School of Thought
1) Unitary by
Centralised
Government
Government Structures of Countries and Territorial Management

Comparison Table of Iranik Alphabet with Dari-Parsi Alphabet

Dari-Parsi	Iranik Capital	Iranik Minuscule	Dari-Parsi	Iranik Capital	Iranik Minuscule
آ	A	ɑ	ز ذ ض ظ	З	з
اَ ◌َ	U	u	ژ	Ж	ж
اُ ◌ُ	O	o	س ص ث	C	c
او	OI	oı	ش	Ш	ш
ای	I	ı	ق غ	Ɋ	q
اِ ◌ِ	Є	e	ف	F	f
وو	W	w	ک	K	k
ب	B	b	گ	Γ	ɕ
پ	P	p	ل	L	l
ت ط	T	t	م	M	m
ج	Ყ	ყ	ن	N	n
چ	Ч	ч	و	V	v
خ	X	x	ه ح	H	h
د	D	d	ء ع	Ɛ	ɛ
ر	R	r	ی	Ɣ	ɔ

Index

Made in the USA
Monee, IL
05 November 2026

67810727R00087